Real

Stories by Shelley Malcolm
Photographs by Terilee Dawn Ouimette

www.marthamartha.net

Real, Second Edition
© 2011 Shelley Malcolm. All rights reserved.

Real, First Edition, published 2010

ISBN 978-0-578-09031-3

Printed in the United States of America

This book is on acid free paper.

Photography by Terilee Dawn Photography, unless otherwise credited.

Cover and Layout design by Live Artfully Productions,LLC

Printed by Signature Book Printing
8041 Cessna Avenue
Gaithersburg, MD 20879

Real

"Real isn't how you are made. It's a thing that happens to you . . . Generally, by the time you are Real, most of your hair has been loved off, and your eyes drop out and you get loose in the joints and very shabby. But these things don't matter at all because once you are Real, you can't be ugly, except to people who don't understand."

—Skin Horse to the Velveteen Rabbit,
***The Velveteen Rabbit*, Margery Williams**

"Blessed are the poor in spirit, for theirs is the kingdom of heaven. Blessed are those who mourn, for they will be comforted. Blessed are the meek, for they will inherit the earth. Blessed are those who hunger and thirst for righteousness, for they will be filled. Blessed are the pure in heart, for they will see God. Blessed are the peacemakers, for they will be called sons of God. Blessed are those who are persecuted because of righteousness, for theirs is the kingdom of heaven."

Matthew 5:3-10 NIV

Introduction

Shelley's Notes:

For as long as I can remember I have been ashamed of the condition of my hands. Shaking someone's hand made me feel uncomfortable and vulnerable. It was as if my hands might reveal a secret. The weathered cracks, the rough skin, now the spots. The embarrassing thought of having a manicure filled me with humiliation . . . I would never have lovely hands like some of my friends.

One morning, I woke up from a dream I might describe as a "reality" slide show of great character and life stories . . . images of dozens of people that I admired. Suddenly, like a personal confession, I was relieved to know we all had something in common . . . the truth our hands tell about us. At that moment, it became clear to me that a deep beauty exists in the honest stories our hands have to tell. Whatever their weathering, in their tenderness, their task, their injury or age, there is beauty.

This book celebrates many amazing people, and their stories celebrate the beauty of authenticity, honesty, hard work, true caring, and devotion. I hope the portraits of their hands and their stories will reveal to the reader an awareness of his or her own genuine beauty. Enjoy and revel. These are real people, reminding us that each of us has a chance to be real and claim our own beauty.

Terilee's Notes:

The moment Shelley told me about her vision I knew that it was something I was suppose to do. I had been praying for over a year that the Lord would use the gifts He gave me in photography for something greater than my own ambitions. I wanted my images to inspire people to love, live, feel and appreciate the unique that is often mistaken for the ordinary. I have often admired hands; the first real photographs I ever took were my dad's. For me, hands have always told the story of how amazingly different our lives are.

It has been a blessing to be a part of something so amazing. Shelley and I walked into the unknown of where this project would take us, and it has changed me forever. I have learned to have courage to understand the deeper side of people. Shelley taught me that. She has been blessed to know people from all walks of life and sees greatness in each of them. She knows their hearts. I hope that through the written and visual stories told in this book, you will find the courage to love deeper, embrace fully, and take the time to get to know those in your life. Everyone has something to offer and so often we don't take the time or courage to seek it out.

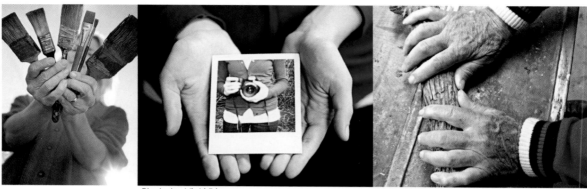

Photo by Vicki Friesen   Photo by Shelley Malcolm

Affirmation:

About the same time as I had this vision and confession, I made a visit to our Minnesota family farmland and stayed with my Uncle Dave, nicknamed "Milty," who is still a handsome, and very spirited eighty "something." He began his challenge with memory loss months before this visit, and changes were becoming more noticeable as time passed. His family had warned me of the signs and to prepare for surprising limitations.

As younger men, Dave and brothers, Ray (my dad), and Bob, had reputations as hard working and incredibly bright, creative thinkers. In fact, Dave had invented and patented several machines and tools that have been used in the tank trucks industry. He also created lifesaving, warming blankets that are used in every hospital today. As a result of his brilliant ideas and inventions, he was able to retire at a very young age; however, he continued to create and design

and build. He would build furniture for his family and friends. He always led the crew whenever the church needed construction. He built his mountain cabin from the raw timber of his land. He was never bored.

It was on the last night of my visit that he took me into his shop where the "magic" happened. The walls were lined with lumber, tubing, and electrical materials. There was a collection of drawings, a few frames, a hope chest, and stools waiting to be finished. Tools were everywhere. It was an organized wonderland of possibilities and memories. As we stood in the chilly, but cozy, shop on this November night he confided, "I know I made a lot of things," and he held out his hands, "but it is sad, because I don't remember how I did it or how I used these tools. That is the hardest thing." Not remembering is a small part of the reality. The true reality is the lasting impact that one person can make on others.

Contents

Courage

Ceo

A self-proclaimed "gypsy," her life has been rolling through the ups and downs with few plateaus in between. She loves when she can surround herself with flowers, color, and beauty. Her mother wanted her to be a dancer, an actress. She herself had been a starlet in her younger years, but as her own star lost its luster, she pressed her daughter to shine as she had. She was a "stage mom." Ceo talks about the hurt and helplessness she felt during her dance and acting classes. There was always a scene in front of the other girls, Mother interrupting what might have been a fun tap class with criticism of her daughter's or the teacher's ability. She would never be good enough, she told herself.

Ceo wanted to paint and draw, to create and decorate. She has a natural talent to sketch and design. There is sadness and regret in her tone when she talks about her unrealized potential. She spent so many years trying to make her mother happy . . . while enduring a bad marriage and raising and worrying about her own wayward children.

As her children turned to their defiant paths, she decided to pursue her own new life. She gave up the apartment she had decorated and drove off with her few belongings. She was free from the past but now concerned for each day and night. She has been living in her car for three years, developing ways to stay clean and well-groomed, even beautiful. She makes wise choices about where she sleeps and how she spends the little money she has. Her recent refuge has been on the merciful grounds of an historic California mission. She dreams about having a better life, and someday decorating another lovely apartment with pride, with freedom and safety.

Kazuo, Vard, Brycen

Kazuo proudly greets his son, Vard and grandson, Brycen. He gently lifts a seedling by the soil and roots. His hands are large for his size. They look strong and younger than his ninety or so years. He may be small in stature, but larger than life in legacy. Kazuo has passed on the values of heritage, hard work and community to his family.

In the early twentieth century, Kazuo's father began farming the fertile land of the coastal river valley. Despite the demands of farming, Kazuo was drawn to the spirit of sports and helped to organize a baseball league among his Japanese friends under the coaching of a local man who was a supporter of the Japanese. Baseball became a tradition and farming became successful; enough that Kaz and his family had their own farm and equipment.

The satisfaction of accomplishment and freedom ended in 1942, when all Japanese were required to leave everything behind and report to internment camps. Not only was Kaz faced with losing his farm and future; his father had been seriously injured in a farming accident and could not be moved. In a tremendous act of friendship, their baseball coach firmly offered to take care of their farm. Amidst constant criticism and prejudice, in an act of great courage and conviction, he offered safe housing to these two men—the last remaining Japanese in the County —at least until Kaz's father was comfortable enough to make the inevitable move to the camp in Arizona. The internment years were difficult, and his father died shortly after their arrival, but Kazuo was able to regain the strength and hope to organize baseball games in the camp. Even in confinement, bonds were made and spirits were lifted.

Upon release, Kaz, like other refugees, was ordered to only seek work in the East. Kaz was one of the few who returned to the coastal river valley, hopeful and prepared for a new beginning. His old land had been well-maintained. His friend and former coach welcomed him home and gladly released the land back over to Kaz so that he could pick up where he left off. This friend from baseball and farming, this friend for life was named Vard . . .the namesake for Kaz' first-born son.

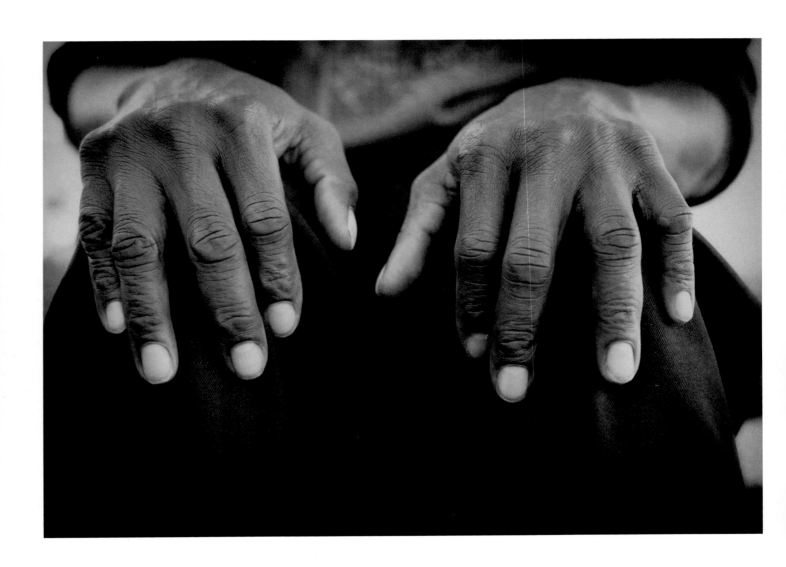

Caesar

Tall and slender with his head held high, he walks with an air of gratitude in each step. His personality is colorful and his presence is full of life. Though his life is simple and his possessions are few, he is a proud man. Caesar's smile is wonderfully broad and bright, despite that he is missing a central incisor.

Caesar is from the Sudan. He does not have much memory of his parents. He was orphaned at an early age during the Sudanese Civil War. He does remember the Catholic school and his fellow students who became his life. As he grew older and began experiencing his own place in the world, he changed courses from attending seminary to traveling the world. In time, Caesar graduated from the University of Turin in Italy. It was here that he began to express his own voice and opinions in writing. The honest perspective that his experiences allowed him to document in his essays exposed some of the terrors of the Al-Bashir regime. Once published, these made him a target of the Sudanese rebel forces. Because of the threat to his life, he was able to obtain an indefinite protective order to remain in the United States. Freedom of speech is something Caesar does not take for granted.

Caesar's willingness to learn and work hard has provided him with a kaleidoscope of jobs, from home construction, to teaching, to hauling, to elder care, to Panda care at the San Diego Zoo. Caesar's life is not only about hard work. He loves to have fun and share good times and good jokes. A favorite story of Caesar's is a night out with the single guys. Terry and Rich took him to the hottest dance spot in town for a night of cut loose guy time. Caesar came home with a trophy for "Best Dancer" . . . a world apart from the Sudan.

Richard

Life is like a fishing line. There is always a beginning and an end, and an inevitable tangle now and then. However, there are also times to cut it loose or straighten it out and try again. The man behind the pair of hard-working hands might have looked at the tangled fishing reel with frustration, but instead he feels nostalgia. The tangles look unsalvageable, but he chuckles, "Yup! That's just about right! This is normal for me . . . I need to get back out on the ocean."

Since childhood, he has had many years of struggle that began with chronic vision problems. He was very well-liked in school, but difficulty in academics left him feeling doubt about his competence. At age eleven, Richard witnessed the traumatic heart attack and death of his young father. They had been camping in a remote part of the Sierras when he heard the gasps for help. His thin, little legs ran more than six miles when he finally was picked up by Lucky, a truck driver. By the time they returned, it was too late. The devastation of being so frightened, helpless, and alone, he will never forget.

He continued to mend his soul from the haunting memories and found escapes in the ocean and mountains. At his mountain refuge, in 1970's Yosemite, he was visited by a series of diverse characters, which inspire the stuff tall tales are about. He hosted people from all corners of the world--nomads, and wanderers, just passing through. It was as if he attracted the bizarre. One morning, he awoke to find one man, dead, face down, in the campfire ashes. Another visitor announced that he was there to end his life as he unpacked a bottle of drain cleaner and bug repellent from his duffle. His world there delivered a new perspective, a new life. Eventually, his own search for healing led Richard back to family.

During successful working years, the pain of the past arose again until it affected his health, work, and his family, but he bravely found help. For a brief time he found a calling as a manager at a rehab home for men and developed a real compassion for those who suffer from the traumas of their addictions and their pasts.

Now he finds peace and reward as a ranch hand caring for horses and other livestock at a "therapy ranch" where disabled and disadvantaged children visit and ride. It is love in action here, as the animals are nurtured, and they, in turn, inspire curiosity, joy, and courage in the children. Richard understands the misunderstood. He offers hope to the fearful, desperate and suicidal. He knows that strength and potential can recover from the most tangled knot.

Jamaine

Along the coast highway, for about twenty miles, she rides almost every dawn. She pedals with steady focus, wearing her warm hoodie and powder pink helmet. The helmet is relatively new. She used to love the freedom of the ocean air in her hair, until the hit and run. Hit on her bicycle, she was thrown off the road. However, this tough-as-nails pixie survived a hip injury, bought a new helmet and got back on the bike.

She is a combination of courage and child-like naivete. Most of her adult life has been spent struggling to overcome tremendous challenge.

She has survived physical limitations from birth, addictions, and homelessness. She has survived the strains that her emotional swings have put on her relationships. She has been the victim of street violence and crime, but appears to be finally coming home.

In the last few years, she has been living near and reconnecting with her family. Even though she is in her 40s, she is accepting the nurturing and guidance of new friends whom she trusts. She is making a home with Rick, a talented musician. It is no surprise Jamaine feels a connection in his home. Here she finds the freedom to set her voice and music free. She has rediscovered her talent on the guitar and is letting it soar. She can play any of their numerous guitars and mandolins any time she wants. She has even, on occasion, played at a local coffee house with her dad and his group. Jamaine may be a little skittish about being tied to a physical address, but if home is where the heart is, her guitar and music make her feel at home anywhere.

Hope

Ken and Mary

They met in a bar. It was not hard for Mary to fall for the tall and handsome surfer from Huntington Beach, who was also a great dancer. It was just as easy for Ken to fall in love with Mary, with her instant, easy laugh and sparkling blue eyes. Ken has always loved to tell jokes, and Mary immediately became his best audience. It has been this appreciation for humor that has lifted them through the years of joys as well as tragedy.

During the early years of marriage, they left Southern California to settle on several acres north of Santa Barbara. With Ken's expertise as an electrical contractor, they began to build their dream home.

Not long after construction began, Ken noticed an unusual weakness in his left leg. Over the course of months it was apparent that the weakness was spreading. By the time their youngest, Krista, was three, he was confined to a wheelchair and had lost use of his legs, hands, and arms. After sixteen years of multiple consultations and tests, Ken's condition remains a mystery. There is, however, no lack of faith or determination on the part of Mary and Ken. They have braved many experimental treatments and traveled great distances with continued hope and belief in possibilities, even miracles. They celebrate each hint of promise including stem cell injections at a Barbados hospital if it may improve Ken's chances of achieving his dream - walking his daughters down the aisle at their weddings.

Under Ken's instruction, Mary and their daughters have become excellent plumbers, carpenters, and electricians. However, the quiet and humble task of finishing their home was kicked up a few gears when the local college discovered their needs. The architecture and construction class chose Ken and Mary's home this year as their community project, improved Ken's accessibility and finished much of the framing, flooring, painting and cabinetry within days. Receiving this generous gift of compassion was a tremendous boost to their silent struggle.

Mary's hands seem to be timeless, strong, capable, and tender. Ken's hands are large, and though they cannot move, one can feel the yearning to share his wealth of knowledge and love, the desire he has to hold his power tools or just a pencil, his wife and daughters, and most definitely the tenacity with which he holds on to hope.

Franco

His truck is armed with tubs, hoses, and the various fluids he needs to make a car sparkle and smell fresh and new. He spends four hours in the driveway scrubbing, rinsing, and steaming. Franco has been doing this for many years. He is proud of his reputation as a automobile detailer and doesn't shortcut his work nor take it for granted.

Franco was born and raised in Guatemala. He was pursuing higher education there and hoped to go to law school. There was much in his life that seemed to discourage that option. This must have been frustrating for someone so ambitious. He moved to the United States hoping to find more opportunity and a better future.

Auto detailing may not have been his dream, but it certainly is something for which he can be proud. His business has created jobs for other young people. He is a role model of gratefulness and courtesy, and practices a high standard of service. As he schedules and details as many cars as he can, he feels happy and excited about one of his dreams which in a few years will come true. "I want to raise my daughter right, for her to be a good person, and for her to go to college. She is eleven, but I am already saving money and planning to give her the most special Quinceañera." His eyes and his smile reflect the joy that this hard-working father receives in knowing that his dedication and perseverance have allowed him to give this to her.

Franco talks occasionally about going back to law school. He shyly questions, "Do you think my accent will get in the way?" He then enthusiastically returns to the job at hand.

Chet

Never married, he is the last in his family line. Chet finds pleasure and comfort in his collections of artifacts and photographs. He speaks with pride about how and he and his brother served in World War II. Even today the drama and beauty of wartime Europe are clear in his memory.

After the war, he was able to go to art school. "Thanks to the GI Bill," he claims. He studied in Pasadena with colleagues of Norman Rockwell. It didn't take long to discover his love for oil painting. His talent allowed him to get a job as an artist and designer. Landscapes have long been his favorite. Visitors to his gallery recognize the scenes with fondness and marvel at his lasting talent.

His vision has dimmed due to macular degeneration. Chet uses this limitation to his advantage and says it enhances his impressionistic style, because he can't see the details anyway. The colors flow with emotion as he touches up another Morro Bay sunset. He is a gentle host during a visit to his home. It includes a linen-dressed table with place settings, warmed rolls, butter and jelly, and coffee. Dozens of framed pieces of work hang on every wall. In one bedroom, his "office," his trusty steel brown manual typewriter rests alongside a modern copy machine.

In the back yard, Chet has his studio. It is small-framed, and sided in wood and clear plastic, which filters the light and keeps it dry and warm. Palettes of color and worn rags smeared with paints are set among the many jars and tubes and brushes. In one corner, he has juice bottles with cuttings planted in soil . . . a miniature greenhouse setting for these promising new plants. This is his palace of creativity. This is where the magic happens.

Chet says he would jump for joy if he were fifty years younger. With a successful crowd of fans and sales, he celebrated a new art exhibit just after his eighty-ninth birthday and is already planning on unveiling his new technique after his ninetieth.

Vicky

A woman's heart is where her passions grow. It is where her joys soar. It is where her secrets rest . . . and wrestle. It is where her emotions ache and her sufferings linger. Her heart is where her hope is restored.

The passions of Vicky's heart are reflected in her home. She is surrounded by creativity, works of art, color, and objects of nature. She finds a peace in the Chumash Indian culture and spirituality. Her heart finds comfort in her dog's company and joy in family memories. Photographs of daughter, Addy, and arts and crafts from her childhood days are everywhere. These reminders are irreplaceable.

Vicky had to live through the most painful loss a parent can face. In 2008, the police came to her door with the news. Her daughter, Addy, had been in an automobile accident. She could not be saved. Everyone who knew Addy immediately imagined the golden-haired, free-spirited girl, who loved the ocean, surfing, and her mom. She had just graduated from high school. It was hard to believe her presence was forever gone. Vicky's neighbors and friends instantly rose above their own heartbreak, and surrounded and sustained her with their compassion. Ordinarily, Vicky is strong, independent, and competent in any challenge. This loss was something for which no one could prepare.

Somehow she has been able to find a way to go on . . . a place in her heart to deal with the hurt and slowly mend over time. Vicky is discovering how limitless the heart is and calls on an indefinable inspiration. She feels Addy's spirit in the sea breeze, the cool ocean water, and the play of dolphins off of the beach by her home.

She keeps her bracelet always as her connection to Addy. It reads: "Forever In My Heart."

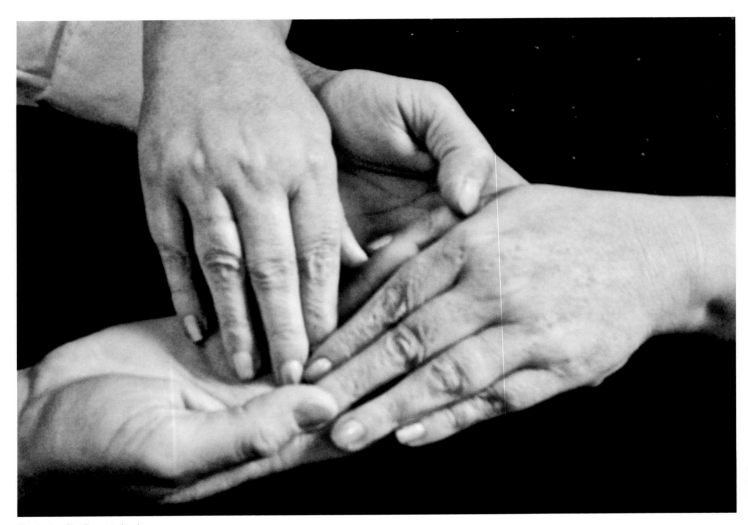

Photo by Shelley Malcolm

Davey and Fran

Davey is a big, tall man, and strong enough to take on any challenge. He is meeting his match. As he lifts Fran's hands to hold them, he is acutely aware of how amazing his wife is but also how weak she is becoming. He has been taking much time off from his long, daily delivery trips for his job. He knows now that every minute counts with Fran and she needs him by her side.

Fran was diagnosed with ovarian cancer in 1995 and has courageously and stubbornly fought back. The illness has affected critical tissues and the treatments have taken their toll. Her body is weary from the insults of the disease, the surgeries, and the needles. The most valuable possession she and Davey have right now is their time with their family.

On this particular day, Fran is dressed for a special occasion. She is in a black-sequined, long-sleeved gown. Davey is in a handsome tuxedo. Having her nails manicured and donning her favorite wig lifts Fran's spirits for this occasion. This is their son's wedding day. They have looked forward to this day with high hopes for strength and health, enough to share the joy of this special time. However, with calm acceptance of her fragile condition, Davey and Fran know that she will be staying home in bed. From the comfort and safety there, she can imagine the smile on her son's face as he sees his bride coming down the aisle. She accepts that this is the only choice today.

She will have time in the coming days to remember with Davey the memories of fishing and picnics, building and decorating their home together, and the fun of driving her sporty little car in the country. It is a time for holding on . . . and letting go.

Renewal

William

"I can't blame it on poverty," William confesses. "My parents were successful in their businesses in Brooklyn." Before high school he had been into much trouble and says that each gray hair his mother has is from each time he was arrested for breaking the law. "Photographs of my hands are a breeze. . . Back then, I was photographed a lot … mug shots… many of them."

William found his way West after he met a "California girl." He is thankful beyond words for the life he lives and the people he meets. Gone are his old beliefs that, "Whites are all alike and to be feared . . . the cause of struggle and failure for Blacks and Muslims." The years of renewal and healing have softened his heart and created a gentler, yet stronger, spirit. His knuckles bear the scars and swelling of the days of fighting and violence, but now the hands are used for greeting, praising, helping, and giving.

William found work at a thrift organization's donation center. He is often heard to greet a donor with a loud, "Hey Brother!" or "Hey, Sister!" His charismatic personality and friendliness have opened doors to lively and lasting relationships with people of all ages, color, and religions. It is a pleasure to arrive at the center as William gives a greeting with a big smile and handshake. He has a passion for US history. Some of his regular "customers" are seniors from the WWII era who love to share their stories with him. One couple developed deep fondness and respect for William. When her husband died, the wife sold his treasured Cadillac to a humbled William for "pennies."

A survivor of a rough past, William, by just being his humble and grateful self, provides a customer with a moment of optimism and affirmation that can turn his or her day around.

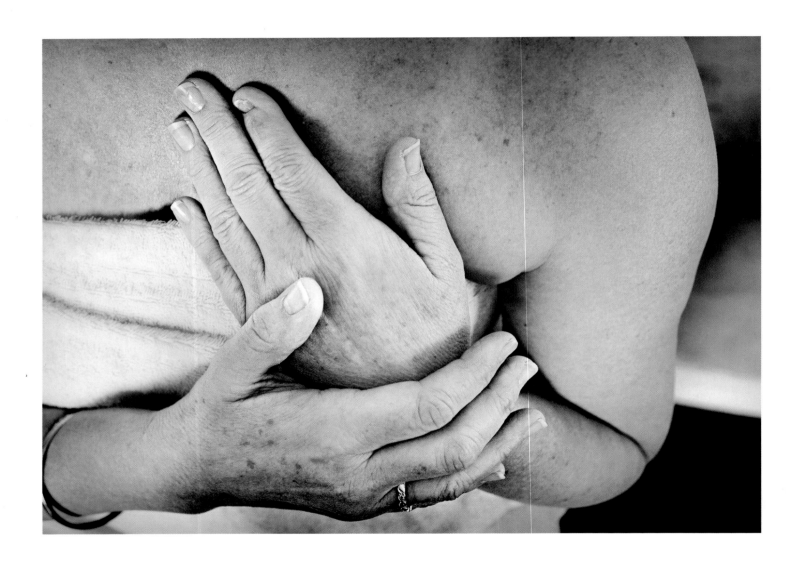

Mary Ellen

As a child, Mary Ellen was the towhead with elfin eyes and mischievous smile. Her safe and simple world crashed at age six when her father died. Her home was still full of love and support, but the anchor of her father's presence was gone. After high school graduation, she tried a few college courses, but abandoned that path with the immediate reward of a paying job. She worked in a variety of positions over the years. Once she became a mother, her sons inspired her to feel that "it doesn't get better than this."

The comfortable routine of working and parenting was short-lived as Mary learned she had degenerative arthritis in her hips. Shortly after turning forty, a hip replacement was necessary. Two years later, she grieved at a familiar pain . . . and the need for another hip replacement. The suffering and challenging rehabilitation caused Mary concern about what was going to fall apart next. The promise, however, of being pain- free, walking, dancing, or skiing again was enough for her to persevere.

There was also the cancer. Preoccupation with work, family, and life in general caused the mammogram deadlines to get lost in the stream of time. The tumor had already created a different texture in her skin. The mammogram and ultrasound confirmed her worst fear. She had a barbell-shaped tumor a quarter-inch from her chest wall. It would require the most radical of surgeries accompanied by powerful radiation and chemotherapy. These treatments would cause systemic changes that would demand the need for daily injections into her abdomen. She was faced with a battle, but cancer found a determined opponent in Mary Ellen.

Mary Ellen has become more fierce and fearless. Her perspective and focus is stretching her beyond her own expectations. She has decided to go back to college and get her degree. Excelling at advanced math and English classes, she is beyond just surviving. She is thriving. She is reborn, renewed, reinvented . . . armed with the knowledge that who she has become is very real. Her new replacement parts have only enhanced this very genuine woman.

Laura

As she takes home another award for her strawberry pie, Laura smiles and reflects on the pleasure her bakery treats bring to others. She now enjoys the rewards of her talents and predictability of her surroundings. Behind her gentle eyes, there is a woman who has been able to heal the old wounds of a life threatening disaster, and the scars are disappearing. Rebuilding her home, her son's future, and her confidence has not been an easy road.

The earthquake is in the past, but on the Richter scale of life events its impact is unforgettable.

On the dark, winter morning of January 17, 1994 at 4:31am, it hit. With the first jolt, Laura shot out of bed, only to see the television bounce and crash to the floor. Immediately, the building was in utter darkness with only the traumatic sounds of smashing dishes, crashing walls and furniture, and the shifting of the floors. She ran to find her son in the pitch-black trap, guiding herself to the doorway of his room. Though the walls were weaving and the floor was cracking, she held onto the door frame so that she would not lose her orientation. She screamed his name multiple times with no response. Finally his voice came through the darkness and rubble. A huge wall unit had fallen between the door and her son. She reached through and found his hand on the other side. The strength of sheer will made it possible to move him through the blockade. Still in darkness, with everything breaking and falling, they decided to try to get out. As they found their way to the hall of the building, Laura remembers the terror as they realized how little time they had before the walls fell in on them. They were the first to be out on the street and soon were followed by others. There was no power. Fires had ignited in other buildings, and everything was in shambles. "It looked like a dump," she describes. The period of aftershocks sent them reeling again into terror. She remembers extreme grief and fear turning to exhilaration the instant they knew they had survived.

For years, the panic would remain raw and immediate. Eventually her sense of impending crisis would fade. Her faith in herself, her friends, and God has found a solid foundation.

Chung

Her name means purity, but she remembers humiliation. Chung was assigned to the "special class" in school . . . the "dummies." Her low self-esteem began to find refuge in solitude. Since her family moved nine times during her elementary years, it was easy to isolate rather than try to make friends.

Chung remembers feeling some sense of satisfaction and adequacy when she discovered her own natural creativity. She found ongoing joy in origami and still delicately folds her favorite birds in tropical and seasonal colors. Music began to reveal her inner voice. She composed her first song at age nine. Chung took pride in her new talents, but she knew they were directing her efforts away from her father's intentions for her. He would eventually come to accept that a medical degree from Stanford, Berkeley, or UCLA was not in her future.

Chung was finding her way. As she pursued graphic design, Chung continued to be discouraged by her struggles with English and math courses. Finally, in her senior year of college, she learned that she was dyslexic. It was a relief to find an answer, and also to find a new group of friends with the same condition who would support and encourage each other. Chung admits with optimism that, "It was not our weakness that defined us. Instead, the weakness defined our strengths."

Now a nationwide magazine publisher, her articles and photos feature the finest treasures and works of the heart. From purses to paintings, sculptures, and antiques, her publication is expanding to cover performing arts. Chung is making her mark and encouraging artists and readers to "discover your passion." By discovering her weakness, she found her strength, passion and freedom.

Dean

"I was a punk kid," he says, "about nineteen years old. I bought a Model A for about $15. My buddy, Slim and I were under the hood when something shifted in the engine . . . At the doctor's office, I kept propping myself up to watch the amputation of my finger, but the nurse kept trying to get me to lie back down. I really wanted to watch."

Most of his life, he worked as an engineer. In his retirement, Dean had been enjoying a new hobby of nature photography. He loved the outdoors and spending time with friends. He was starting to have some difficulty with breathing and overall discomfort. On first examination, an inhaler was recommended for asthma, but it wasn't long before he learned treatment would require more than an inhaler. With no hesitation, the physician said, "Your heart is no good." He needed a heart transplant and had little time. Dean's age dictated the quality of the heart he was eligible for: a "Grade B" heart or "alternative heart."

February 13, 2003 the call came. A heart was available. The donor had been exposed to Hepatitis C and was qualified as an alternative heart. To Dean it meant his new heart, his life. After a pause to talk to his wife and accept the reality of the moment, they immediately prepared for the long drive to UCLA. Since the ride might be his last, he wanted to go in style. Joyce packed everything they would need into the trunk and back seat of Dean's convertible Mustang. Upon arrival at the hospital, his old heart was beating its last.

His surgery began immediately. For two weeks Dean remembers his disbelief that the transplant had even happened. When he finally saw the radiographs, which revealed the wires that held his ribs together, he was overwhelmed with gratitude for this miracle. His new heart may not have been first rate, but Dean has been restored. Like the old Model A, he's got plenty of miles left.

Joan

One of the most impeccably dressed women in her retirement home, Joan enjoys a challenging round of bridge. She is a commanding threat to her opponents. It is a perfect arena to exercise her intelligence and love of the game. Lately she is enjoying the creative writing groups. The new opportunities are refreshing to someone who has endured difficulty for so long.

Joan's future was uphill from the beginning. Her mother suffered from mental illness, and Joan recalls the hurtful echo of "life would have been better if you had not been born." After the divorce, her mother kidnapped her. The abuse she suffered at the hands of her mother, stepfather and uncles only worsened when she was infected with polio at age fourteen. Her ailment was debilitating. Despite a year of hospitalization she was left with major deformity and disability.

Despite her childhood wounds and handicap, Joan found strength and confidence in her intellect and eloquent social skills. While working her way through school, she soared to the top of her classes, received scholarships, and graduated Phi Beta Kappa from college at age 19. She did not let the difficulty of walking or having a non-functioning arm get in the way of socializing, looking fabulous, or finding romance. She married her engineer husband and would soon enjoy motherhood herself. She was aware of the challenges she would face with only one functioning arm. During pregnancy, she prepared by lifting and carrying heavy bags of sugar or flour. She redefined the term "single-handed," as she changed diapers, fed and clothed the babies, and created a beautiful home. She made it seem so natural that even her sons did not realize the feat. Over time, hard work and post-polio weakened her legs and she needed the mobility of a wheelchair.

Since the death of her husband, after forty-five years of marriage, it was obvious she would need assisted care. Her experience at her retirement home has been one of success. Joan can enjoy meals, games, entertainment, and even the beauty salon. Her room is arranged so that it is easy to dress for the opera or work on the computer. She may have limited use of only one limb, but Joan will continue to "seize the day" with a wholehearted grip.

Work

Amy

Petite and athletic, with sunny blonde hair, the ocean sparkle of blue eyes, peaches and cream skin, and gentle but spunky smile, Amy looks like a modern-day Tinkerbelle. Her voice is soft and reserved, and her words well-chosen and effective.

Born in Wisconsin, and living much of her young life in the Midwest, she is now a "California girl." She has developed a passion for the ocean and the outdoors, especially the sport of surfing. She relishes the lifestyle of her beachside college town. Working in a winery allows her time to surf and truly enjoy the outdoors. The winery experience enhances her love for beauty, nature, and celebration of life. Special occasions, the gathering of good friends and family, and music are most dear to Amy. She has organized truly memorable times, which are often a combination of innovative idea with old fashioned fun . . . like the private rock concert at a vintage chapel, with beautiful linens, photography exhibit, and an all recyclable, bring-your-own, picnic box dinner.

Amy is a powerhouse of a young woman. She is beautiful and strong. Her size and appearance contradict her potential and ability to get a job done. Her crew has tremendous respect for Amy and her standards, and they follow her lead. She works alongside them in her lace-trimmed camisole, work boots, and leather gloves. Amy is a vintner. She successfully runs her own vineyard and winery, and has a growing reputation for her "ancient vine" zinfandels. She often begins the harvest season days in the dark, cold morning hours and ends them covered in dust and sweat. During these weeks, her fingernails bear the rich red stain of the juice.

Her young hands are, for the moment, resting . . . enjoying the fruits of her labor, the dormant season, and time to relax with her dog. It will be only a few weeks before the beginning of new vine growth signaling another season to work hard and celebrate.

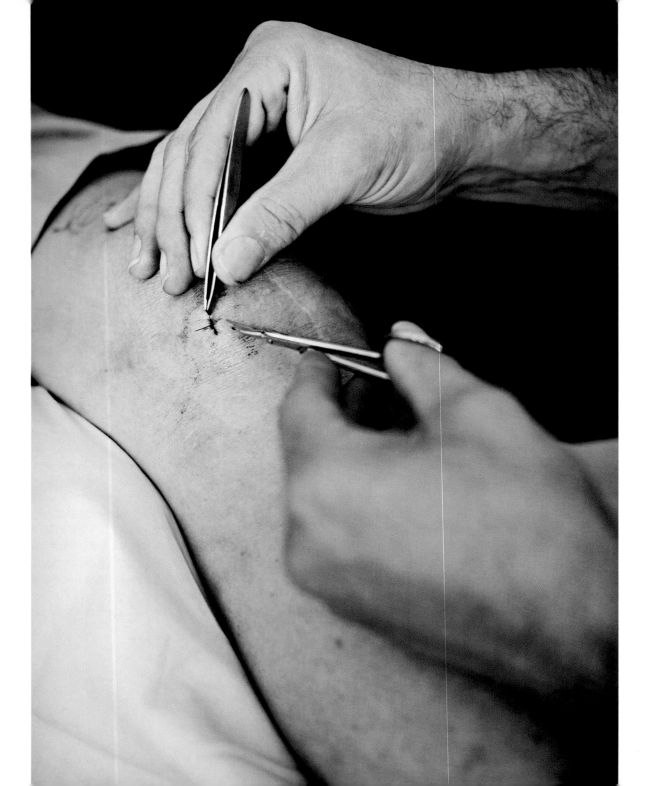

Douglas

Finding his destiny and his mission has been quite a ride for Douglas, and it seems like he is looking forward to much more. The oldest of three energetic brothers, his mother was disabled and struggled to keep up with her growing boys, while his father worked long hours. Doug devoted himself to school, sports and scouting . . . To this day, his Eagle Scout award means more to him than any other achievement.

In high school, a near-death experience from a car accident brought Doug to a deeper sense of direction in his life and abilities. To look at his resume, it appears that he expects a lot of himself. The truth is, however, he loves what he does and has no regrets. He seems to thrive on very little sleep . . . "increments of 90 minutes," he claims; "three hours is nice." Intellectual pursuit has always been his lifestyle. He has accomplished more in his education and with his degrees than most people. Doug's first degrees were in engineering, but after a few years of working, and

a life-changing train-hopping experience from Oakland, California to New York, he decided to go to medical school. Emergency medicine was his calling. It was a natural setting to focus his adrenaline reserves. In his forties, he decided to go to law school and now successfully practices both law and medicine.

His hands have held a human heart, a newborn baby, and a Styrofoam cup of water that he used to baptize a dying person. His hands have gone through the massive stacks of records in legal cases. His hands are often at the wheel of his airplane flying from one deposition to another or on the wheel of his camper van, which allows him to sleep on the road after a night in the ER.

His hands have held the hands of his wife, who is the most understanding and independent woman he will ever know. His hands are steady and confident because even if he doesn't know all of the answers, he'll turn over every stone to find out.

Tom

It used to be tie-dye Friday, but now tie-dye is everyday. He says the colors make him feel happy. When a person works as hard as Tom to make a living, it may as well be fun. Running his own liquor store business in a small neighborhood is his life. It is a family operation, with Jen and Ashley behind the checkout. Tom is on his feet all day long and rarely comes out from behind the deli service counter. He has become the "king of pastrami," and fans of his concoctions come from north and south to get their sandwiches and hot dogs from him. His signature PLT with New York pastrami is a favorite. Everyone who walks into his deli is immediately greeted with a larger-than-life welcome, like he has prepared the fatted calf just for them. No longer are they a stranger. They have become a friend.

It is hard for customers to resist a scoop or two from the ice cream tubs. There are many flavors.

Taste testing is allowed. For some of the locals, it is a tradition to walk up for ice cream. One man approached the familiar corner sign with his preschool-aged granddaughters, and with excitement the girls spelled out, "L . . . I . . . Q . . . U . . . O . . . R. . . . ." Then came their proud announcement, "That spells ice cream!!!!!!!!!!"

Tom works from sun up to sun down. His willingness to listen to his customers and make someone else's day better seems to be drawn from a well of boundless energy and optimism. If he ever has a bad day or is feeling weary, he must keep it to himself for when he gets home. As he hangs the closed sign on the door, he knows that his dedication is worth it. Customers will return tomorrow for a feast of treats, colorful conversation, and fun.

Maybe there is magic in tie-dye.

Brian and Terry

Rarely seen without his aviator sunglasses, shredded visor, and five o'clock shadow, Brian is the older brother. He made sure Terry knew who was boss during their youth. "I trained him well… made him stronger." Brian's demeanor is rugged, yet his presence is gentle. The sunglasses are a reminder of his recklessness as a kid, "from staring at a solar eclipse for too long with no protection." A devastating and lasting injury, which dislocated his spine from his sacrum in his young adult years, has deepened his character. The persistent pain is expressed in his creativity. His passion is art, using canvasses of torturous color and darkness to reveal deep emotions and his private past. He is constantly working, claiming his body hurts worse if he slows down. Time is spent between teaching art classes and construction jobs with all too occasional brief escapes to his own artistic projects.

More reserved, Terry has an extremely diverse work resume, which keeps him in constant demand for building construction and automotive service, seven days a week. He is young enough to still realize the value in his options and goals. He hopes to get his degree from the police academy, but makes his daughter his priority. Having become a father at age eighteen, he devotes his work and free time to her even more since she, her dog and cat have come to live with him. The added presence of a wide-eyed young lady in their home has given the brothers a new perspective of themselves.

These two brothers are different as night and day. It is their differences, however, that allow them to work together like peanut butter and jelly. Although their hands boxed and bruised each other as children—and they joke that they still do—Brian and Terry have a refreshing drive and the strength of a small army to finish the biggest of projects. There is diversity and surprise in their projects as they take on anything from remodeling retail shops, to designing and building massive sets for theater and opera companies – creating bridges, train stations, Japanese shojis, prairie churches, even the Holy Land. These two men share endearing and approachable spirits that promise, no matter how different they are, they can overcome differences, work together, and support each other. They are brothers.

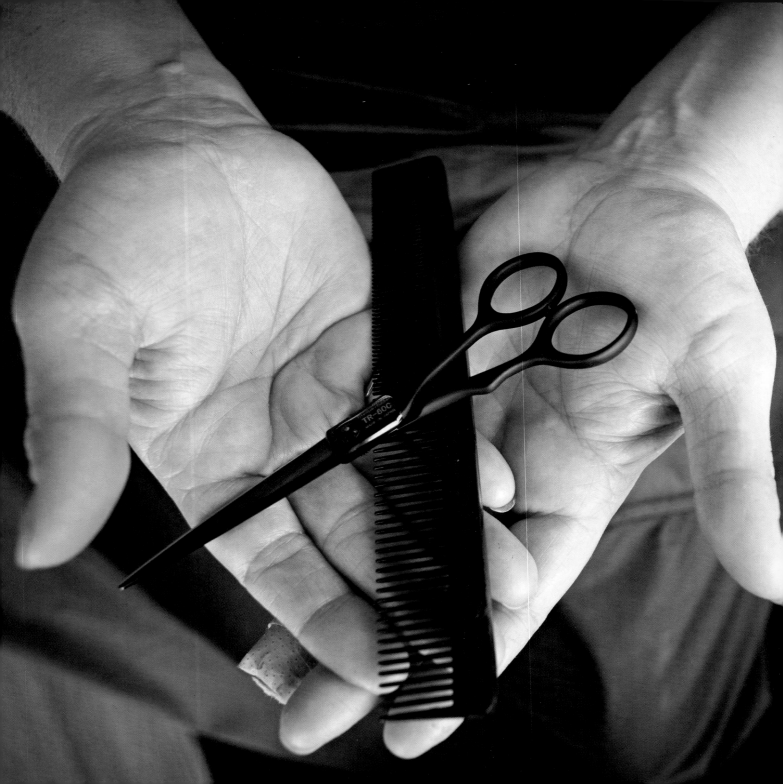

Shelly

One of high school sports' greatest fans: volleyball, soccer, football, baseball, she loves it all. She has an open enthusiasm and supports the players and their teams. Anyone can hear the latest scores and statistics by taking a step inside of her beauty salon.

The chatty buzz is positively effervescent in her parlor. There is always much discussion about what is happening in the high school sports calendar that week. Occasionally a student, coming from school, will pass by and greet Shelly.

Sometimes men stop by for a trim or shave, but most of her clients are women. In the Village, newcomers are not strangers for long, especially at Shelly's, one feels like family. Shelly knows everyone by name.

The salon is beautifully decorated with a clean and modern style. The warmth of the colors, the fun displays of products and trendy accessories make it easy to wait for a turn in the chair. It is not easy, however, to resist buying a pair of earrings or glitzy reading glasses. The energy in Shelly's salon is so cool and fun that it almost feels like being part of a Steel Magnolias. It is amazing how this woman can multitask. She can be running off the stats of the weekend, ordering take-out lunch, directing a vendor to drop off a product, while she is coloring and trimming the latest style. She does not miss a beat. With radar ears, she picks up on a name, or topic, and keeps the room chatter going with a cheerful and sincere attitude. She is supporter, encourager, and wonderful listener.

It seems as if there are no bad days at Shelly's, only bad hair days that become better in every way.

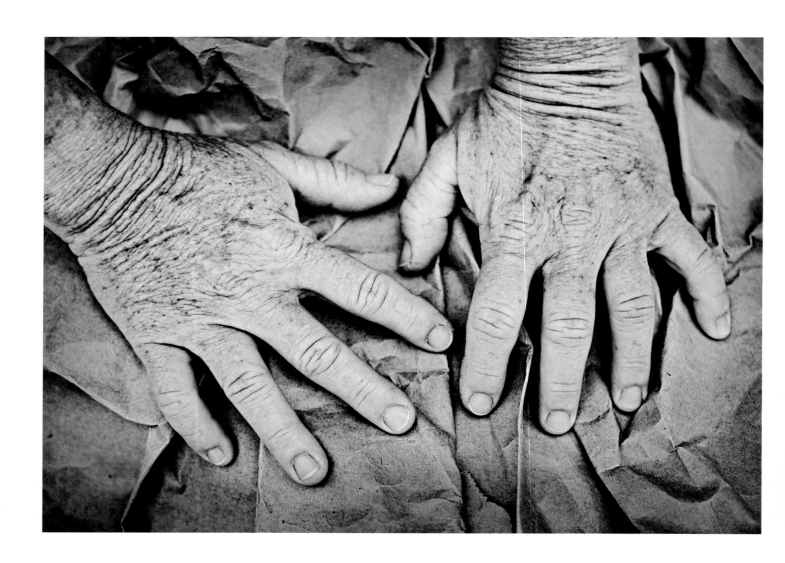

Candy

Going boldly where no one else wants to go . . . there is no storage unit too cluttered, no closet too trashed, no estate sale too overwhelming, and no dumpster too intimidating. It is Candy, the high priestess of organization. The former nurse and dedicated mother has become a superhero. She wastes no time in taking action.

Life got busier during her daughter's early years, and she was determined to prevent chaos from leading to disaster. Candy discovered great satisfaction in planning and putting things in order. As she began to help friends arrange and rearrange their homes and offices, she realized her innate ability to coordinate available space with lifestyle patterns. She helps them de-clutter and create more efficient storage. Candy was transforming their "chaos into calm." Before long, she was receiving calls from a church leader to help with an attic, a theater director to help with costume and props storage, aviators to help with their airplane hangar, and many elderly to help with their estate sales. It is a pleasure to see the thrill in her clients' eyes when they see the beauty of efficiency that wasn't there before. The stress of burden and dread is relieved. Even the job of sorting out the treasures is relatively painless. Candy, in her insightful manner, sifts through it all with those who find it hard to "get rid of stuff." Occasionally, a client will just turn the job over to her to do her magic, but most often they enjoy the motivation they gain from working alongside her.

She has been encouraged to write a book about her methods. It is her attitude and energy that would be hard to duplicate. When Candy sees the piles of clutter as the garage door opens, she may be found to say, "piece of cake!" or "ooh!--this is gonna be great!" as she boldly goes where no one else wants to go.

Dreams

Genae

A vivacious twenty-something, Genae giggles as she anticipates her best friend's twenty-first birthday. Her eyes and smile grow wide with excitement as she envisions the planning and decorations. The same, broad smile returns when she breaks into song, a voice talent that is good enough for a musical production or just singing in the car with friends.

Because of stresses in the economy, Genae knows she is lucky to have three jobs. She has very little free time, but at least she can pay the bills for now. It may not be long before she loses one or more of her jobs. She worries about her friends. Instead of going to movies, they meet at coffee houses, and instead of the gourmet cappuccinos, they get a small daily brewed coffee or an ice water. The conversation is rich, and is a bonus in the midst of compromise. Many of her friends have had to move back home with parents or share incompatible living situations. It is a hard time to dream beyond the next day or week. The friends encourage each other and persevere with an optimistic spirit. Seldom is Genae without her generous smile and an outstretched hand to help others. She is selfless, an inspiration.

Genae can find simple pleasures in each day, even though times are hard. She and friends will make up their own silly entertainment, like quoting Pride and Prejudice, talking in animated accents, and randomly painting only one fingernail with the color of the day. By remaining hopeful and creative, having fun and understanding friends, the worries are less overwhelming. She is of the young adult generation who will inherit the world. They are here to contribute and to succeed. The generation of Genae has arrived.

Aaron

Dashingly handsome and charismatic, Aaron has had a passion for his art since early childhood. The wheels of creativity and imagination are in gear most of the time. When he talks about a project, his whole presence lights up. A dreamer of big dreams, he has the maturity and vision to see beyond the initial concept of a story. He is a trained and educated professional and does what it takes to make his dreams become a reality.

Aaron's early stage and television acting experiences seem to have been a preview of bigger things to come. As a child, he toured the United States as young Gavroche in the musical "Les Miserables." Television and film have been added to his resume.

Early in his career, a serious auto accident caused injuries, slowing him down for a time. The back pain still haunts him, but his determination rises above any limitation. Aaron's incredible versatility, ambition, and competence allow him to be constantly busy directing for film and stage, teaching eager students, writing scripts, filming, and producing his own projects.

His standards are high, yet his manner is thoughtful, humorous, patient and fun. Like a child on his birthday, there is an undeniable sparkle in his eye when he gets an idea. In his hands as a director, the ownership of responsibility is very visible. His hands wave and point with expression as he guides his actors through scenes. Every tiny phalange muscle works as he rapidly writes or types his notes. The intensity of his vision is seen in his hands, as fun as it seems to be, he is not just playing around. He is ready for "Action!"

David

At sixfoot five inches he casts a confident shadow. However, when it is time to board another flight, he is always thankful for the aisle seat. Usually his travels take him thousands of miles from his Solana Beach home to the beaches of Spain, Tahiti, Hawaii, Barbados, South Africa, and other destinations people associate with paradise.

His job sounds like paradise, but it is often high-pressured work that goes into double-digit workdays. David is a producer/filmmaker of surfing documentaries. He may have to grab his gear and fly out after he is notified that a swell is coming into an island off of Mexico or sleep extra nights on a palette in a South African village because conditions delayed filming of a surfing event. He is young. He is single, a surfer, a filmmaker, and he loves it.

Water is David's element. He was swimming before he could walk. At age four, the thrill of catching his first trout was the beginning of a new world. David had his fishing pole rigged and ready to grab for any trip in the car, at the remotest chance there might be a stream or pond on the way. His first job was at the live fish market on the pier. The commercial fishermen would bring the day's catch to the market and David, wearing his big apron and knee-high boots, would sort the fish into tanks, weigh and even clean them. It was not long before he even ran the cash register and made change . . . he was not yet thirteen years old.

With his love of the outdoors and natural academic talent in the sciences, his parents thought he would certainly become a marine biologist. However, David continued his passion for the ocean as he directed his career to photography and video production. He inspires others to follow their dream, It is as if the stars were aligned just right and he has won the prize, but he confesses that he must keep his standards high, beat the deadline, keep learning, and work hard. As David follows his heart . . . the ocean, fishing, surfing, friends, art and fun . . . the passions of his heart follow him.

Meredith, Kelly, Carly, Trevor and Mike

Part of an extraordinary class of high school graduates, these young people were motivated in every way. They loved the challenge of academics, sports of all types, the arts, the youth group meetings, and mission trips. They were active in extracurricular activities, clubs, and volunteer work.

They had developed a bond of friendship that became the catalyst for this motivation. Each friend encouraged, supported, or challenged the other. This dynamic made their daily routine seem more of an adventure. Even preparing for the SATs or filling out college applications was a bonding experience. Their friendship appears to be as wholesome as a script from a 60s television show. It is, however, as real as the smell of chocolate chip cookies baking in the oven.

These friends are now in college. They have been the high achievers of high school and behave as if they expect nothing less on this level. They plug in healthy doses of fun, humor, and silliness as needed to balance the demands they put on themselves. They keep each other in check with their cell phone messaging. It is like passing notes, with the ability to respond in an instant.

Their idealism and confidence are paired with a healthy balance of wisdom and accountability for their young age. Their world is changing rapidly, and they are prepared and armed with all the tools they can gather, including each other, to move into the age of adulthood.

Robin

He sits on the step of the broad back porch, next to a rocking chair. His loyal chocolate cocker spaniel, Lily, crouches patiently and protectively at his feet as if Robin's wellbeing is her mission in life . . . " I just always wanted to play baseball," he simply confesses.

Growing up in an All-American small town, he remembers his growing love of the sport. By high school it was a lifestyle and becoming a part of his identity. Robin went on to play baseball in college and beyond. His passion and talent eventually led him to the major leagues. He was becoming a star. This star only got brighter and stronger as his career turned golden, no less than six times, with the Golden Glove award. Robin has batted left and thrown right for Chicago, New York, and Los Angeles.

He has realized his childhood dream and at the same time developed a future. He and his wife, Stephanie, moved and traveled through the years of big league play and eventually settled in their dream hilltop home. In addition to their children, Robin and Stephanie have made their community their family. They open the doors of their home to various large group meetings, Bible studies, and celebrations.

Robin has supported school and community sports. He has readily responded to the needs of others including victims of the 911 tragedy. He and Stephanie are major contributors to the newest cancer center in their area. This facility will offer cancer patients the greatest prospect of dealing with their illness and prognosis with dignity. He has realized his dream and is helping others achieve theirs.

His other dogs clamber up to the porch, happy to be a part of this family and community. Life is full for this grown boy who just wanted to play baseball.

Balance

Betty

Betty, also known as "Doc," inherited a love of nature, the outdoors, and horses from her photographer father. As she followed her father's footsteps, they paired up to work on film projects including Disney's earlier nature documentary films. Eventually, her love of animals drew her to veterinary medicine. She has taken care of animals on the Central Coast of California for sixty years. On the family property, a hospital and house are nestled away from the street near a creek and woods. It feels like home, because she spends most of her days and nights there. She occasionally makes the break down to her beach house for a night and morning reminder of her real home, where her neighbors are glad to see her. If her car is noticed in the driveway, a neighbor might bring a cat or dog over for a quick consultation. She is patient and accommodating. She talks about getting the kayak out, but doesn't remember when she last did.

Betty seems tireless. She has cared for countless animals and spent many sleepless nights with illnesses, traumas, and births. She is THE Doc on duty. Her staff is loyal and very supportive and hardworking, but when they go home at the end of the day, "Doc" stays with the animals as needed. It frequently is a twenty-four-hour-a-day job. There is no room for being squeamish here, as she calmly collects the black drool from the swollen mouth of a rattlesnake-bitten Labrador . . . as she attempts to resuscitate a stillborn puppy . . . or, as she, in her deep and experienced wisdom, comforts an owner when it is time to "let the old dog go."

It is a blessing that Betty still loves adventure, because it is the traveling that revives her when she needs it. She travels with camera and gear to the Galapagos, China, Hawaii, and Africa with the enthusiasm of a college student. The stories of Betty's travels are anything but sedate and restful. Getting shot in Africa and sharing a good whiskey are among them.

Here is a dedicated woman who is the "real McCoy." Her pearl-buttoned, plaid western shirts, bolo ties and pocket protectors are her signature style, as are her Ford Bronco with her dogs, her parrots, and camera gear. One can imagine her riding off into the sunset, like a western movie, but it is not time for that yet.

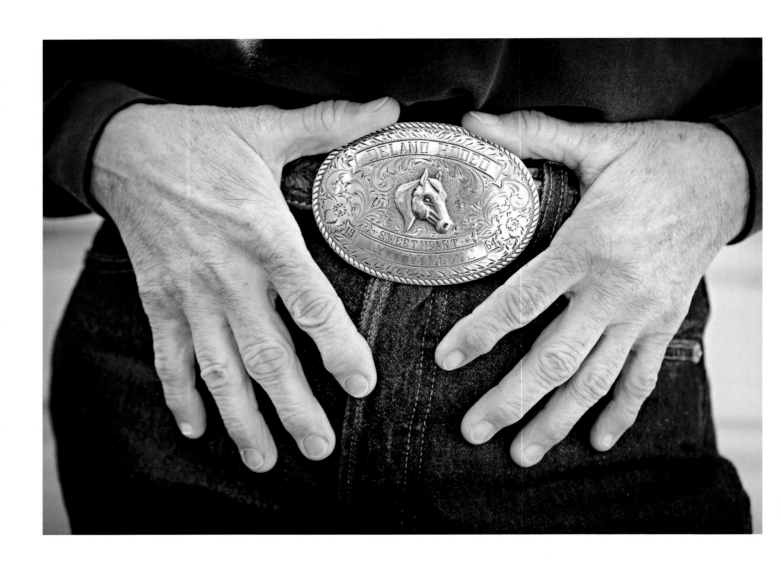

Lynn

Zipping along the tree-lined road in her sparkling black TR6, Lynn is as fun as she looks. She is trying out a new "subdued," semi-retired lifestyle, but it is hard to keep a good cowgirl down.

Since the mid-1970s she has worked with all the big names: Brad, Leo, Gwyneth, Oprah, Matt . . . Now the glamorous, fast pace of her Hollywood photo agency has changed to allow her more time to enjoy her valley horse ranch and the serenity of her cottage at the beach.

A woman who "talks the talk and walks the walk," Lynn is in her element as she arranges a photo assignment for television's "America's Next Top Model." The former Rodeo Princess is just as at home while "freeze" branding her horses. She is comfortable on the seat of her Harley or in the old wooden pew during church services. Lynn loves to deliver gifts of homegrown lemons or fresh-baked coffee cake to volunteers at the hospital. On her "to do" list is to renovate an old boat and take a Spanish class.

As varied and full as her life is, she holds fast to the elements that endure. Her family ranch has taught her the beauty and rituals of birth and death, as she has delivered newborn foals and cradled two of her old dogs in their last days. She has learned strength from her favorite tiny life form, the acorn. Lynn has gathered and planted them knowing only a few will actually grow. The mighty oaks that make it will bear witness to Lynn's love for them, her horses, dogs and family.

As she travels her triangle between homes, her constant pal is Thomasina, her Australian shepherd. They are usually in the big Yukon and heading for a new adventure or deserved rest. As she cruises up the street to her beach house, Lynn hangs her head and arm out the window to wave to neighbors with her fingers positioned in a peace sign. Here Lynn can "semi-retire" until the call of adventure beckons her once more.

Jane

It is an unexpected image to see Jane's nails in a natural state. No polish, no color, and just one treasured ring on her finger. She has enjoyed a glamorous life, inspiring one to wonder what it might be like to have lived in her shoes.

Her career in film began with attention to her beauty and famous, voluptuous figure. She had talents that allowed her to enjoy successes in acting, singing and dancing for decades. She is beloved and held enduringly as an icon, as a one-of-a-kind.

On the surface, one would imagine her story as one of celebrity, glamour and pampering. The deeper story is more impressive . . . a commitment to a cause that is greater and more lasting than the world of celebrity. She is devoted to her faith, the power of prayer, and the needs of children.

Jane has held regular Bible studies in her home for years. She has served on committees to support prayer in public settings. Jane has prominently voiced her opinion on the rights of the unborn. She is fearless and committed. Her devotion to the needs of less fortunate children created an organization that has found homes for thousands over five decades. In the 1950s, her mission to help orphans of war became a foundation known as WAIF. Jane's remarkable strength and tremendous love continues to aid children all over the world.

Jane has balanced a contrasting lifestyle. She still dons the sequins and jewels, and is a glamorous presenter for the SAG awards. In the same week, she draws an audience as a singer and entertainer at an upscale resort. Her fondest times are spent serving up a casual lunch for her small town friends at her home after heads have been bowed in prayerful thanks. She fulfills the expectations of the public, while fulfilling her honor to her faith. Her talent, ability to commit to diverse efforts, and beauty are extraordinary and rare.

Cathy

Paddling out on her longboard at Malibu seems to be a memory. A Malibu surfer girl, Cathy is tall, blonde, and athletic. She still has a love for the beach and the sun, but has moved north to her mobile home in a little beach town where the water is colder. The move was a chance she would take on her business. In her heart she knew it was where she needed to be, near her brother, who was facing surgery on a significant tumor. It was hoped treatment and therapy would allow Bob, who was always athletic and fun, to regain his health and an active life. Cathy wanted nothing to get in the way of her support for him. She gave up her thriving Los Angeles based agency and began working from her mobile home office, hoping she could balance the needs of her brother and serve clients to keep her business going.

Thankfully, Bob has recovered to the point of being able to surf again. Content to keep her home near him, Cathy is immersed in her element ... the art of connections and casting. In her office, she is surrounded by computers, keyboards, fax machines and, of course, the telephones. Over the years, her right hand has begun to tighten up in spasms. Her grasp is weaker and keyboard work is not as easy, but business is nonstop and she is thankful for that. The office never closes and messages are received at all hours of the day. She doesn't waste a minute. In the film casting business, communication, and timing is essential. Cathy has been doing this for decades and still loves the adrenalin rush of discovering a new "star" and connecting actors to an audition. She loves the dreamy ambition of newcomers, and of being the vehicle to launch them into their film careers. It is this dedication to her clients that keeps her tethered to her phones and computers.

Someday she may trade back the keyboard for the surfboard; for now, she is happy to know her brother is riding the waves. She is connected; life is good.

Danny

Sitting in the doorway of his RV, he is resting and pleased with his progress. After a long day of heavy moving and hauling, it is his joy to come home to set his inner artist free. Danny is finishing another of his large vehicle custom paint designs. The sky is the limit when he presses the paint sprayer. The universe with all its glory is his signature design . . . its planets and stars in infinite layers of blues, pinks, silver and gold metallic cover all surfaces of the van. Even on the interior, he has tended to detail. His vehicles are a masterful blend of art and love.

Danny loves to create. He says it is the freedom of his artwork that helps him survive and endure the most difficult trials in life. He finds solace in attaching a T-shirt scrap as a sail to the soldered masts of a mantel-size pirate ship. He becomes thoroughly immersed in the watercolor of a landscape, and a torch-cut copper bust of Jesus.

Danny has great pride in being resourceful. "One man's trash is another man's treasure," describes his ability to turn salvage into beautiful jewelry or wall artwork. He has an eye for potential value and beauty in a discard, which, once transformed by his hands, becomes a work of art. In preparation for a local theater production, Danny's own appearance was transformed during the rigging of overhead props. The large, tattooed man, with Jerry Garcia hair and beard, sleeveless T-shirt and biker pants, had to ride his motorcycle home, covered in glitter, sparkling, on his sweaty skin.

Danny is kind, and his swollen fingers reveal that he goes the extra mile when he works. Once at home, with the workday behind him, he allows himself the freedom from the rules, to trust his heart and his hands— following his natural passion is his gift to himself.

Wisdom and Acceptance

Gladys

Her fingers are taking a shape of their own these days. At times, to use or move them is painful. She can still write a letter and occasionally she can piece together a jigsaw puzzle. She enjoys reading her Bible; however, her interests are more than sedate. With the excited energy of a sports fan, she looks forward to golf tournaments on television and loves to keep up with the stats of her favorite players.

Gladys has strong and fond memories of the earliest days of her local Lutheran church. It was in that church that she found her calling, one to which she was devoted. She took on a range of responsibilities and held multiple church positions before she ultimately became the designated writer of notes, acknowledgements, birthday greetings, and thank you cards.

She brought to the task the training of her Midwest education, and a self-cultivated discipline and commitment to continue practicing impeccable penmanship. Her skill exemplified "the art of letter writing."

The perfect lines, loops, and cursive lettering of her early notes appear almost like fine lace—an art form of her own design, delicate and beautiful. Her handwriting encapsulates a legacy of excellence and attention to detail that somehow, in its perfection, still exudes warmth and love. To hold her hand-written note is to experience grace and beauty.

The flowers and trees outside her sliding glass door are her daily entertainment. There is pleasure in witnessing the small changes of the seasons and the sounds of the birds that bring the outdoors to Gladys. She is homebound with physical limitations, yet she is far from bored. She has learned the art of slowing down and doing less. Life is simple and visitors are treasured.

Heather

She looks fair and youthful, with a hint of innocence. Heather has been able to retain those elements of her character alongside the obvious presence of her "old soul." As a preschooler, with unique energy and joy, her world of play seemed so vivid and fun; it was easy to accommodate an invitation to join in. The look of "knowing" in her eyes revealed something deeper inside. It was as if she'd been born with a great portion of imagination and grand intuition. As she matured, this intuition became a little scary for her, in that she began to sense a darker side to situations and people. It was awkward to possess a certain bit of wisdom at an age when children are naïve and carefree. Her gut would tell her something, but she was too young to express it or know how to handle this extra "sense."

There were times when it was too much for this little girl, and she would be overcome by fear. With the understanding and support of loved ones, Heather found ways to explore these feelings and learn to trust her inner voice; she sought ways to use this intuitive sense in a positive way to help herself and others.

Heather is true to herself and accepts that not everyone needs to understand. She has an incredible faith and welcomes this ability of discernment. It has not only made her comfortable with herself, but also fearless and incredibly compassionate toward people who are hurting and alone. She is somehow able to connect in a very nonthreatening way with people who find themselves isolated and misunderstood. She is the best friend you ever had. Nothing you say could make a difference in her caring. She has a love for the genuine and for the hard truth. These are the hands that have gripped in fear, prayed for a friend, held the hands of a loved one, rested in wisdom and acceptance, and confronted the darkness.

Heather continues to find great joy and release in music and creativity. Her strong, versatile singing voice and impeccable comedic timing seem to contradict the deeply sensitive and intuitive persona offstage. The truth is that the childlike playfulness and energy has never been lost. She has found the key to wisdom and depth of character combined with freedom and joy.

Carol

In the closet, the stacks of writing and poetry have gotten taller over the years. The words on their pages silently sit, in waiting. Some have been stored for decades, and some have never been shared. Carol is often inspired to write. However, most of her energy is balanced between family and her work with the wounded and hopeless.

For years she has been a counselor and spiritual leader. One of her therapeutic programs is based on her own philosophy that uses a metaphor for life's challenges. She calls it "stones for the journey." Using "stones" as symbols of human needs such as security, empowerment, and individuality gives her students a tangible basis for understanding and expression. The journey is of self-discovery, to find the "gem" in one's self. Carol believes that each person has his or her own "luster," it just needs to be discovered and appreciated. She is a strong teacher who possesses gentleness and patience, which enable her to lift clients from the depths of emotional devastation and trauma, to hope and healing. Their voices begin to be heard, and their luster to gleam.

Her own journey continues, and Carol's inner poet, like a diamond in the rough, is calling on her courage to share the words of her writing . . . to let it shine. She looks at the stacks of poetry and hears, "You can do something with this." It will take time and courage, but some of her poetry will finally leave the closet.

Eileen

Praying is a regular exercise for the hands in this portrait. It is one of patience . . . of love . . . of years of enduring . . . years of faith. The years are apparent in her hands, but so is the story of her childhood and her youthful, romantic dreams of marriage during wartime.

Eileen is one of ten children born to Thorjus and Emma. A farming family in Minnesota, her parents discouraged speaking their native Norwegian as it was not respected and was considered less intelligent in their community. She remembers sleeping three siblings to a bed, and waking up to frost on the ceilings in the morning and the smell of bread baking in the kitchen. She remembers the excitement of roller-skating and how she and her sisters had to share the pair of skates. If two sisters wanted to skate, they would each wear one and happily roll along. There were sleigh rides, church picnics, gathering of eggs, and singing harmony to "Shine On Harvest Moon" while washing dishes.

At age eighteen and in love, she married. After a precious few weeks, her husband was sent to battle in Germany. Tragically, he drove over a land mine in his jeep. It was more than fifteen years, after a move out West to California, before she loved and married again. They quickly and happily had three children. Once again, tragedy struck and the life of her husband was cut short . . . too young for a heart attack. Eileen picked herself up and persevered with optimism and hope and devotion to her children and God.

Even though she is at a time in her life when it is becoming difficult to hear and her vision is minimal, she is happy, at peace, and content with God's plan for her. She has wondrous hopes for her children and grandchildren. Even at age eighty-nine, her role as a mother continues.

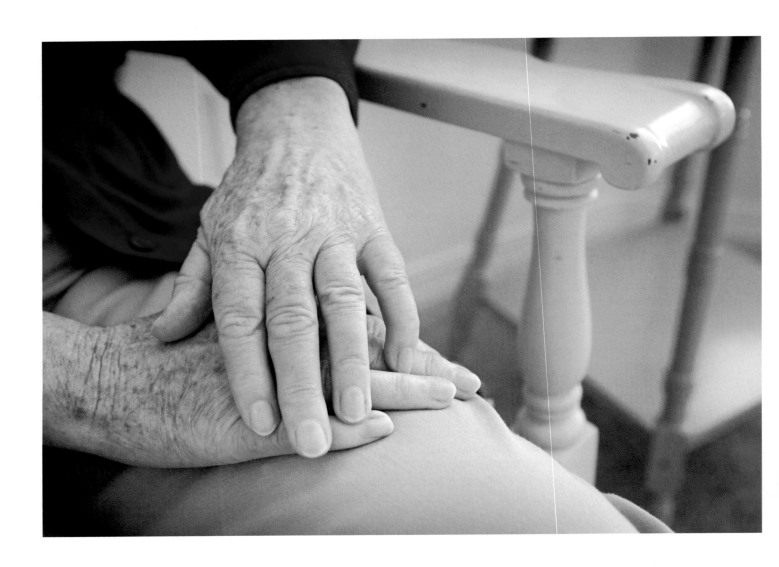

Sheila

Suddenly the rug gets pulled out from underneath and things will never be the same. There is reason to cry, scream or blame when things go wrong or seem too hard. Grief and anger can linger. Sheila has been there, and somehow found peace and a safe place to land.

She and husband Larry had six children in as many years. Larry's work took him a day's drive from home. The busy demands of a large brood made her look forward to his times at home. Their dreams were just beginning to unfold. One morning, Larry left for work and would never come home again. She got a phone call. Larry's truck was in a horrific accident, and he had been killed in a fiery blaze. Her children gave her reason to embrace her life, to have hope and faith, and to persevere.

She possesses an unhurried grace. With a very calming presence, Sheila has earned the key to simplifying life and securing a place and time for serenity amidst turmoil. She has learned the benefits of acceptance and tenderness. The activities she chooses nurture her soul. In turn, she finds she can continue to devote time towards helping others. As she has begun her eighth decade of life, she lives alone in her seaside home. She volunteers at the community hospital, church, and food bank, but makes sure to reserve time to drive to see the wildflowers, to walk on the beach, and to have lunch with a lifelong best friend. Mostly soft-spoken, she loves a good laugh, especially at her own Irish heritage.

She raised her children, survived the tragic loss of her husband, and even survived cancer. Cancer seemed to hardly register on her Richter scale of trauma. She has been through the worst of fires and knows that it is wise to courageously move forward. Sheila chooses peace.

Kallie

The headaches had become so debilitating that it was common for her to miss school. Once the pain hit the only way to deal with it was to shut out the noise, light, and movement, and wait. There were even "blackout" moments. Migraine was the diagnosis and she would manage the pain with medicine and rest. Many days were spent in isolated pain.

Concerned friends gave Kallie a gift of a quilt with hand-tied yarns. There were sixty knots. Each knot represented a prayer for her healing and freedom from pain. Three days after she received the quilt, she had a headache episode that changed her life. At a musical practice, she felt strange, and went outside with a friend. Immediately, she began to have a seizure. Upon emergency medical assessment, she was flown to UCLA, where a vascular mass was discovered at the back of her head. It would require surgery and her great courage to proceed. After removal of the initial mass, and with further treatments,

Kallie's headaches were gone. Her future was about to change.

The need to be fearless has not dampened her angelic presence. She has been able to maintain stability with epilepsy. She has found support from others afflicted with this challenge. Canaan, her beloved guide dog, has helped her adapt to visual impairment. Her optimism and courage have turned her into a leader. Kallie travels the country lecturing and visiting others who share her ailment. She encourages children and young adults through difficult recoveries. Kallie is a frequent volunteer for Make a Wish Foundation. One of her greatest pleasures is working with Recordings for the Blind and Dyslexic.

It is mystifyingly appropriate, but on several occasions, others, even strangers, claim to have witnessed an "angel" around Kallie. Kallie's path may at times have led her into darkness, but she is an example of light in the darkness, which has only gotten brighter.

Inspiration

Lois

These are the hands of an inventor . . . Lois has always had the creative sense with the mechanical. She has also had a fascination with the human hand and how it functions. It seemed natural that she would become an occupational therapist specializing in hand function. She invented a prosthesis, which would improve life for those with hand disabilities.

Retiring to her beachside residence, Lois has the most beautiful and colorful vegetable garden. She loves to work the soil and tend her crops. She collects the rainwater in her homemade cisterns, and is one of few neighbors who rarely fill any bin but their compost or recycle cans. Her garden reflects a certain harmony with the earth for all to see. She usually has an abundance of fresh-cut flowers for the taking in a bucket. Next to it is the recycled gallon milk jug labeled "Clean Dog Water," with a happy dog paw print on the side.

Lois found another calling in restoring function and life quality to a new client. When her dog, Peta, was rendered paraplegic, Lois created a cart system, which allowed her canine pal to roll along happily for years. It was not long before she was getting calls from dog owners who also hoped that their dogs would be mobile again and live a better quality of life.

For her own pleasure and curiosity, Lois spends many hours in her workshop with her wood-carving tools, strings, springs, and motors. She has become a master toy maker. Her delicately designed toys are out of the simplest materials, yet incredibly complex in their function. They are whimsical, but absolutely genius. She has ducks that waddle, dogs that run and wag their tails, a man drumming as his head nods, even a dog milking a cow as she turns her head. Many are brightly painted, while some are natural wood. They are works of passion and patience. It is with pleasure and quiet humbleness that Lois works away. Her hands have worked tediously for tens of hours to complete even one toy. She recently chose a favorite toy to donate by the hundreds to school drama programs. Her invention is a wind-up pair of hands that applaud for several minutes. This toy should have been made for Lois. She deserves the applause, maybe even a standing ovation, for her amazing gifts that make this a better world.

Daniel

It was a job that nobody wanted to do. The sewer line under the old woman's house had been crushed to the ground, settling over years. She could not use her plumbing until it was fixed. After snaking a video camera under the house, the destruction was found. The only way to repair it was to redo the sewer line. Outside the house it was easy—cut the concrete and dig down to replace it.

It was the part under the house that looked impossible. Because of the raised foundation and location of the damage it was concluded that someone would have to dig a trench from the outside. The trench would have to traverse at least twenty feet and be excavated to depths at more than three feet deep. Plumbers arrived with their big trucks and equipment ready to rescue, but when they saw the difficulty of the trench under the house, their fees rose to an outrageous figure. It was obvious that this was a job they didn't want to do. The only way was to dig by hand under the old house with whatever tools would work. The cost would be prohibitive, because the hand-digging could take days, and sewage would be encountered.

Then a friend recommended Daniel. He arrived and did not hesitate . . . nor question the difficulty of the job. He ignored the sarcasm of the other crew and donned the borrowed wetsuit, which would help to keep him warm. He dove under the house and slowly, steadily, and carefully dug with his hands and trowels. He would come up occasionally to unload some of the mud and muck from his bucket. Since the house was built over a spring, the constant water needed to be pumped out by the other crew. As they watched Daniel come out of the impossible hole, the other men would smirk, "I would never do that job for under $17 an hour." It took two days of nearly impossible work under the most difficult conditions. He emerged from the trench for the last time, happy that he could be of service.

The old woman's plumbing was restored and she gave a homemade medal to him for his heroism. Daniel was, deservedly, paid more than he had requested. There were a handful of neighbors who asked how he could do it. Daniel's immediate response was, "God made my hands for praising, for service and for work. I do it for Him."

John and Anne, Lloyd and Sandy, Kris and Dana

Sharing a home, and much of their lives, with each other, these three couples have a daily routine that involves an early morning bus ride, a full workday, dinner, and an evening walk. Sometimes the entire group walks together with their pugs, Rocky and Reggie. Sometimes they walk in pairs, always greeting their friends and neighbors along the way with joy and enthusiasm.

A hug or a handshake from them feels like love . . . unbounded, happy, and sincere. Each married couple truly loves each other and expresses it without reservation. They are eager to share the secrets of their happy marriages. "Love each other no matter what," say Lloyd and Sandy, who just renewed their vows after eleven years of marriage. "Love each other always," say John and Anne, the most senior of the couples, married over thirty years, "and love God."

They care about their community. When they had an opportunity to speak in front of the city planning commission in a group effort to save an old church building, they did not hesitate. Each spoke carefully, thoughtfully, and emotionally without concern for the television cameras. The permit was approved and the church was saved.

They travel frequently, to places like Hawaii, Las Vegas, Disneyland, and the mountains of California. Lloyd has even been to Japan. Sports take them to these places. They are athletes and champions in the Special Olympics. They are excelling and having the time of their lives at an age when many adults are looking at retirement. They proudly let their medals shine. They are heroes in Special Olympics, heroes in their community, and exemplars of true friendship.

Kim

Tall and willowy, her ivory skin and red hair give Kim an almost fairy-like presence. Fifty years of wood floors and mirrors . . . the dance studio and the stage are two of her workplaces. The other is her home.

At home, she is surrounded by color. Hundreds of costumes—from silky goddesses to elephants-- in colors of the rainbow and metallic aliens to fluffy pastel tutus hang from the rafters. Bins and shelves of fabrics and accessories sit waiting for their turn to become one of Kim's creations. Bundles of yarn and spools of thread in fuzzy blues, violets, oranges, greens and reds are displayed on racks on walls. This expanse of creativity and productivity takes tremendous organization. It is a wonderland of color, texture, and potential. Her surging and sewing machines, and costume racks are never dormant.

Dancing, sewing, knitting, and teaching are her life. The days are full, yet she still has time to lovingly tend to her family, which includes tortoises, cats and Tango, her dog. Her dance shoes show the wear and use from a lifelong passion. Her body, from head to toe, feels the aching years of dance, but still finds the joy and pride in knowing she's "still got it." Her hands have gone the extra mile — expressive and strong through their days and nights of designing, fitting, and creating costumes, and knitting bunchy warm winter goods for friends and family. Kim beautifully "colors" the world in her quiet, diligent, dancer way.

Randy, Patty, and Erica

Randy and Patty's hands cradle the brave fingers. Over several years they have lifted and carried, guided and taught Erica. She has learned patience and understanding, trust from love and encouragement, and respect for herself and others.

Erica was born with cerebral palsy and was facing a critically limited lifestyle. Her natural parents decided to accept and trust the dedication of Randy and Patty to give Erica the full-time care and training that might allow her to have hope for a better quality of life. They all have witnessed miracles at work in her years of therapy, surgery, education and socialization.

Having raised their own family and four other foster children, Randy and Patty find the source for their love, strength, and caring for others in their faith. Randy, a church pastor, fire department chaplain, and Patty, a special needs teacher, are humble, kind, and selfless. Their record of service might be a book of its own. They inspire a deeper conscience to be a better person . . .to go a little further, be more patient, and love a little more . . .especially love the unlovable. They are dedicated to those in need, each other, and to God.

Through the willing hands of Randy and Patty, Erica is realizing a life full of interaction, opportunity, learning, and the courage to keep on trying. Her joy and laughter are contagious. The lively blonde teenager has celebrated another big birthday. Just like all teenage girls, she has her favorite styles and colors, movies, foods and friends. Under Randy and Patty's care, Erica's spirit, courage, and self-discipline have built a foundation for launching into her future. Holding fast to God's hand, they have been able to persevere, cry, laugh, and know fully that the world is a bigger place when they look beyond themselves.

Purpose

John

Dedicated to honor, dignity and freedom, John is a knight. He freed an imprisoned King, and returned him to his empire . . . the King of Beasts, that is. His story is the substance of fairy tales, and it is real.

He smiles as he remembers the lion's tremendous power, sharp claws, and teeth. Handling the affection and play with even a young lion required wise caution and great strength. Years have passed since they took him home, but the memories are strong.

It was 1969, London. The hip, young Aussies, John and Ace, were right at home. They were usually seen in bellbottom pants, neck scarves, boots, and the long and shaggy hairstyle of the Rolling Stones. Their lives were about to change when they discovered an extravagant pet shop in a large department store. As they watched the irresistible cub through the pen, it did not take long to decide to take him to home to their modest apartment above a furniture shop. As Christian, the Lion grew, supplying adequate food and space to play presented big challenges. John and Ace soon recognized the young lion's need to be set free in his natural African environment.

Under the guidance of lion expert, George Adamson, arrangements were made for Christian to be moved. He was able to adapt to his new environment and others of his own kind. John and Ace worried about his transition from the life of a city house cat to King of the Beasts. In a dramatic meeting in 1971, John and Ace visited the lion's new home. They were told that they would be lucky if they even saw him. The huge beast would be unpredictable, potentially dangerous, and most likely would not remember them. Christian did come into sight and bounded towards John and Ace. His final lunge turned into a deluge of massive furry hugs, nuzzling, and kisses. His enormous size was overwhelming, but his affection was genuine and familiar. The reunion was recorded and has been viewed on video by millions. Christian never forgot how much he loved his boys. Love is full of surprises. Love has its own language.

For years of service to conservation as Trustee of the George Adamson Wildlife Preservation Trust in the Zoofari Committee of Taronga Conservation in Sydney, the Royal Geographic Society, and Elsa Conservation Trust, John was knighted in 2005 as a member of the Order of Saints Michael and Lazarus.

Suzanne

Her hands are decorated like a Christmas tree. Each piece of jewelry is chosen and placed for its own special reason. Suzanne stands out in the crowd and she is adored. She has a boldness of spirit, style, and fun that is contagious. The shock of spunky red hair, brightly colored or animal print clothing, and jewelry are her trademark. She has a passion for studded and rhinestone purses and furry boots. She brings out the kid in her friends.

A true free spirit who follows her heart when it comes to caring for people, Suzanne has a very deep sense of compassion and continually gives her time to others, to listen and pray, and to hold up those who hurt and struggle. She is comfortable reaching out to a stranger, and her combination of wisdom and sense of humor allow her to minister in unique ways. She has recurring roles as Raggedy Ann in the area hospitals, as the Queen of Red Hats, as the Halloween Nun, as the Makeup Artist, and as a Sunday school teacher. For over thirty years she has proudly and gratefully held the hand of many caught in the throes of addiction.

When it is time to not be so serious, Suzanne is free and fearless. At a dance class for mature women, she redefined "mature" as she danced to ABBA's "Dancing Queen" while wearing a leopard bra over her leotard and sequined bellbottoms. On a recent Valentine's Day, she arranged a private proposal to her husband of thirty-five years, at a local chapel with the theater lights glowing a warm red, and a Harry Connick, Jr. CD playing "Only You" in the background. "Of course!" was his reply as she gave him a newly-designed wedding ring. This was not the first of her romantic surprises; she once sent him on a "treasure hunt" where he was the "Man in Black" looking for the "Lady in Red."

Suzanne's grandchildren are among her most enthusiastic admirers. They know in their grandma they will always find a nonjudgmental ear, an unhurried lap, a delicious blend of wisdom and silliness, and inspiring surprises which will teach them to simply be and love themselves.

George

The high-tech job at IBM seems like another planet away from the George most people know.

His hobby has become his mission; his beautiful precision carpentry has become his legacy. George has lovingly and painstakingly designed, built, and finished countless works of art and furniture. While building his own home, he has willingly volunteered his talent on spiritual and community levels. The communion railings, the lectern and pulpit, and majestically lighted cross were built by the skill and strength of his hands and inspired by his faith. He accepted a request from a local community theater to build stage props. George's wood shop became the laboratory of the imaginative and whimsical, from coffins to a school bus. When the dance studio needed ballet bars for their little "Twinkle Star" ballerinas, George made time to prepare and install them ensuring they were comfortable and safe for their little hands.

A visit to George's shop is a treat for the senses. His favorite music plays softly on the radio. The hot pot for heating water, mugs, and packets of hot chocolate are readily available. However, this is a serious carpenter's workshop. The massive tabletop is the centerpiece. The perfect organization of specialized tools along the perimeter reveals the purpose of the time spent around it. Best of all is the scent. The pure, sweet fragrance of sawdust fills the room gently and invitingly. George is frequently asked during a week, "What project are you working on now?" His most ready reply is, "More sawdust!"

George is a tall, strong man, however, when he speaks of his loved ones, he frequently gets teary-eyed with fondness, pride, or concern. He claims a constant optimism . . . the secret might be his favorite food, peanut butter. He has his mantras. When asked how he is doing, he is never anything less than "incredibly well!" His favorite Bible verse is stamped in many places around his home: on his sidewalk, at his desk, in his shop . . . Phil 4:13 (I can do all things through Christ who strengthens me.) With his faith, tender heart, and large precise hands, George has the right tools for any job.

Terri Lea

She is a small-town girl with a head and heart of gold. Terri has a presence that is as natural as the morning sun. The sparkle in her eyes and her smile, and the wind-tossed, wheat-colored hair could be described as homegrown, or "farm fresh." Her family farms some of nature's most treasured produce: avocados, strawberries, Japanese cabbage, and sunflowers.

Terri is a woman with a grateful heart. She realizes that "to whom much is given, much is expected," and she willingly serves on the local and global levels. She is an organizer and a leader. Even when her children were young, Terri was volunteering. She inspires others to participate, whether it is decorating for a graduation, serving food to the homeless, or running a marathon.

Terri beams as she shares her excitement about her beloved Kenya project. She initially helped to build homes there, but returned home to continue support through sending funds from proceeds of her private business, and by the sale of beaded jewelry made by her Kenyan friends.

For her recent birthday, she took twenty-eight girlfriends out of their comfort zone to raft down the mighty Kern River. They all braved the river, because of their love for, and trust in, Terri. They survived to tell tales of sharing sleeping bags in the freezing night under the meteor showers, the dangers of flipping rafts, and Terri's birthday cake presented by the rugged rafting guides who were dressed only in aprons and their own birthday suits.

Occasionally, Terri makes time for herself away from the dynamic of leading the group. She has a passion for her service as a Hospice volunteer. She loves her dogs, her family, and the quiet of her rural home. If love and encouragement are the seeds she sows, her life is yielding a great bounty.

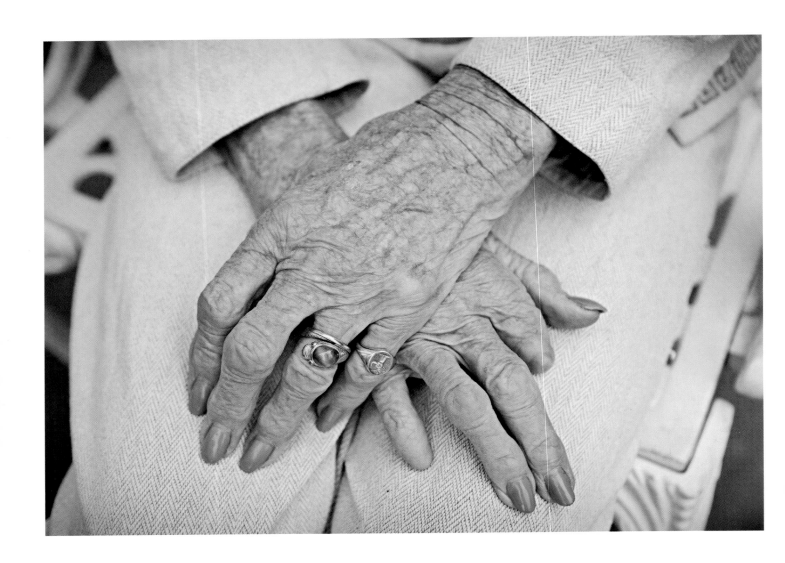

Eve

Meeting over tea, on a drizzly London spring afternoon, she has breezed in from Japan, looking composed and fresh. Her silver white hair, cheerful eyes, and warm smile greet us. She looks crisp and comfortable in her white linen suit. Her handshake is vigorous and genuine.

Her life seems "supersized" for the small package she comes in. She had been a modern woman since her early years. Describing her time as a glider pilot, "I had to pretend to be a boy so that they would let me learn," she confesses. Comfortable with daring adventure, she fondly talks about the thrills and narrow escapes, in her solo flights.

Eve has passed this spirit on to her children and grandchildren as she continues to support their pursuits and dreams. Her family, particularly her son, is recognized for bold and inspiring achievements on land, sea, air, and globally on a humanitarian level. Her son appropriately named the first stratospheric passenger aircraft after her, the mother ship, Eve.

Over the last two years, Eve has had a growing devotion to a number of villages in Northern Africa. Upon a visit to Morocco, her associates discouraged her from visiting a village that had aroused her curiosity. Despite the warnings, she approached the young women there. She found them suppressed in their environment, with very grim futures. On the first visit, she introduced the skill of knitting to three girls. Immediately, they fell in love their new craft. They were able to create beautiful items to sell in the market and found great confidence in their productivity. The interactive program has grown. Now a business, the program has provided funds for construction of schools where they can learn and work. Eve has found that as the young women are motivated to help each other, there is hope for their economy and future. Continually reaching out to the villages, Eve recently brought Scottish cashmere goats to the area. As the goats breed and thrive and more jobs have been created.

Asked about her missing fingers, she describes a trip downriver in England. She and her husband were delivering a barge to their son. At a point near one of the locks, she got out to tie-off the barge, momentarily, and as she had the rope secured around the cleat, the barge suddenly went into reverse and the rope wrapped her fingers tightly. She pulled her hand free but the fingers were beyond saving. When asked if the missing fingers on her right hand create limitations for her, her response is immediate, "Not at all!" It seems there is nothing she can't do.

Life

Steve

Steve delivers. Through the pelting rain, in the heat of the sun, past the barking dog, up the steepest hill, nothing stops him from delivering the US Mail. He has been as regular as morning, never failing.

Walking the streets of the same neighborhood for decades, he has seen just about everything imaginable. He has delivered birthday cards over the years to children who suddenly are old enough to be waiting for him to deliver their college acceptance letters or RSVP's to their weddings. He delivers the good news and the bad news. Steve has delivered congratulations in one week and then cards of sympathy in the next. He may be the first to hear a reaction to the news, because of his consistent daily presence.

Since Steve delivers mail right to the front door mailbox, his recipients seem to look forward to greeting him. He has become a friend, especially to the elderly people who live alone or rarely get out. He pauses often, and for several minutes, to hear about their latest visit to the doctor or their newest grandchild or great-grandchild. His manner is earnest and patient. It seems no story is unimportant to Steve as he listens, even after walking for hours, he stands and listens . . . because he believes in what it means to these friends. He is willing to share the sorrows and the laughs.

The hum of his truck, steady rhythm of his footsteps, and the creak of the mailbox lid are comfortable and happy reminders of the predictable routine of the day. His mailbag gets lighter as he passes off the bundles, and of course, he will return the next day. Steve, the mailman . . . regular as morning.

Jonny

It was with a bit of daring and whim that we decided to get the cartilage of our ears pierced. Of course the potential for pain was a factor, but the intimidation I felt about going to a tattoo parlor was another obstacle for me to overcome. My three daughters insisted that this shop was the best in town.

Jonny met us and gave us forms to complete and asked for the required identification. In addition to his multiple tattoos and facial piercings, Jonny's nonchalant demeanor had me curious.

"Before we actually do this, I need to know something." I asked, much to my daughters' embarrassed groans. "Are you happy today? Are you in a good mood?" He looked up and spoke sincerely, "Yeah! I just got back from a vacation and you are the first customers today. I am rested and happy. This will be easier than you might think."

He took the four of us into his workspace, which, besides the artwork and cluttered décor, looked much like a dental office, complete with autoclaved instruments, sterile materials, and sparkling stainless steel. This young man took his work seriously and treated us with sensitivity and deliberate care. He talked us through the procedure, step by step . . . "the needle goes in as you exhale . . . it will be as smooth as a knife through butter."

Jonny was extremely hygienic, changing gloves, materials, and tools with each person, checking for blood vessel anatomy on each of our ears to be sure he had marked the correct spot. As each of us stood up with our new earring, and attentively listened to Jonny's post care instructions, we were so relieved and proud!

Tattoos and piercings may be at the peak of popularity, but Jonny's manner reminded us that etiquette, patience, respect and daring never go out of style.

Jim and Garin

She was supposed to be a boy, a Gary, hence the name Garin. The name is as unique as she is. She seems unaware of her beauty. Jim is a man who needs few words to be heard. Standing six foot seven, he is a commanding presence. She and Jim love their privacy; however, they are continually involved in community efforts. They are known for their generosity and support of the arts and education, and they have helped to resolve difficult and sensitive public issues in an efficient and positive manner.

Their home is in the country, but the rural feeling surrounds their law office in town . . . a large restored vintage house with shade trees on spacious grounds. For awhile, there was a charm to the clucking of the hens and baby chicks that would scatter across the lawn. Garin enjoyed finding the precious warm eggs that were regularly laid under the bushes. She was worried that because they were not confined to a chicken coop, that dogs, opossums, or other predators would find and destroy them, so she would check each day to rescue as many as she could. She was unafraid of the watchful mother hens who at times chased or pecked at her. She wanted the babies to be safe.

The chickens were choosing not only Garin and Jim's yard, they were beginning to spread through the main street. They were colorful and friendly, and became an attraction to visitors. At first glance, they were a reminder of decades gone by. As traffic brought more visitors to the nearby lake and wine tasting at the vineyards, the chickens were getting in the way.

From the beginning of the "chicken zone," cars began to line up for blocks while a chicken dawdled in the street. The drivers had to be cautious: a flock of chicks might follow from the curb. There seemed to be an endearing tolerance for the chickens, until pedestrians and automobiles became endangered due to chicken distraction.

Then Jim stepped in. He loves his wife, but he holds no fondness for chickens. He knew how much she cared about the chicks, but it was time to put safety first. It was time for the chickens and egg-laying to come to a stop, even though he knew that their presence would be missed. The solution was a win for everyone, including the chickens. The hens were moved outside of town and only roosters were allowed to remain. The early morning "cock-a-doodle-doo" announces harmony and that the streets are safe once again.

Photo by Shelley Malcolm

Peggy

We had arrived for our four-day trek along the Inca Trail to Macchu Picchu. As we loaded our luggage into the shuttle at the Cusco airport, we were filled with the anticipation of immediately exploring the ancient city's streets and shops. The air was cool, yet comfortable and the skies vast and clear. It did not take long to realize how thin the air was at this elevation. At our lodge, Peggy ushered us in and immediately perceived the ambition in our eyes. She wisely advised us of the perils of high altitude sickness. She welcomed us into the parlor of her lodge and explained how important it was to have a cup of coca tea and lie down for at least a three-hour nap. "It is then that you will be ready to see the city of Cusco!" she cheered.

Peggy was petite, and we noticed she wore her extra layers of clothing and a big alpaca overcoat to keep warm, even indoors. This week was a particularly difficult time for her as a hostess, because her Peruvian father had just passed away and her family was coming in for the week. She apologized for not having much time to tend to her lodge guests, yet it was still easy to get to know her in the limited time we had.

Explaining that much of her life was spent in Switzerland, she decided to settle near her father in Cusco. She spoke of her father who had lived his life the jungle area outside of Cusco. He had mined the river for gold, often to find pieces of extraordinary size and value. She spoke with such pride and love for this man whose presence had meant so much to her. She was most proud to wear the gold rings on her fingers . . . each designed as an individual hand cast in gold from her father's precious trove.

Photo by Meredith Malcolm

Robert

"We are closed on Tuesdays," his voice, like Sam Elliott's, softly came from under the black cowboy hat. "Open tomorrow though." It was Robert, with his striped pearl-buttoned shirt and red bandana. The only person at the pack station, he was breaking up the salt blocks into smaller chunks to portion out between the horses. He was glad to have a break in the quiet routine of chores and directed us to a counter where we could reserve horses for the next morning ride.

His shoulders were broad and posture strong, but his graying mustache and hands promised that Robert had been a horseman for several decades. From his hat to his boots, his entire presence blended with the leather and rope of riding gear in the tack room, the post and rail fencing of the corrals, and the warm beauty of the horses.

Robert talked about his early years of backcountry trail rides and hunting trips with his father.

As vast and dense as the forest and mountains are, he is comfortable and at home there. He talked about the recent rain and how great the pines smell after that. He knows the peaks, passes and creeks. He knows the seasons and cycles of nature. As he described backcountry hiker rescues, wildlife and the coming of winter, it was easy to imagine the ruggedness of the mountain life. As if painting a scene out of the Old West, he explained that the station would be closed and secured before the snow and the horses would have to be moved to lower elevation as they wait for spring.

The horses whinnied and nickered as they watched Robert leave their corral for the reservation counter. They pawed the dusty ground curiously. They knew he would be bringing their food the minute we were gone. The next morning Robert, on Bull's Eye, would lead Trigger, KC, Ginger, and Whiskey as they carried us into the high Sierra frontier.

Ray

A soft-spoken gentleman, Ray's career as an accountant had spanned more than four decades. He was deservedly proud of the work he did. His attention to the details of calculation and record-keeping was impeccable and satisfying. A nicely-pressed shirt and slacks, and his polished shoes reflect the care and attention his wife, Georgia, gives to Ray. She would be sure that, when he went out the door, his silver-white hair was carefully combed in place.

It was natural that someone so detail-oriented would adapt his interests to a hobby so tedious and focused. Ray discovered his passion for vintage radios upon retirement two decades ago and continues to work on one everyday. He has restored hundreds of them. He is ninety-three years old and plans to renovate radios for years to come. Motivated by his love for productivity, he is rewarded with the pride of bringing these artifacts of a bygone era to life.

Grandson, Nick, admired his grandfather's favorite pastime and how Ray enjoyed the mess it could make. He said he couldn't remember when his grandfather's fingernails were not stained from the layers of wood stain, varnish and oils. However, when it was time to clean up or guests were coming, Georgia was sure Ray did what he needed to leave hardly a trace of grime and dirt. The hands would become clean and his beautiful ring replaced on his finger, as if both Ray and Georgia agreed on a time to play and a time to be proper. He knew that it was worth cleaning up, because there was rarely a day without sitting down to one of Georgia's famous desserts . . . over sixty-seven years with the love of his life.

Love

Woody and Kay

It was a surprise romance . . .

Woody had just lost his beloved wife of six decades to a chronic illness. His love was so great and enduring that, as wise and faithful as he was, it was the hardest thing he'd ever done, continue on without his Marguerite.

Along came Kay.

Woody and Kay had been childhood friends from age three through elementary school, but it had been decades since they had seen each other. They both were happy to have remarkable memories from over 80 years earlier. They remembered making mud pies and catching bugs, neighborhood games and beginnings of school. They remembered the wide-eyed excitement of making perfume in jelly jars with water and rose petals. When they met again they were both widowed and welcomed this spark of love and comfort.

It was only weeks after this reunion that they decided to get married. Woody was seeing the world again in a joyous light. He was happy and hopeful, respectful of his love for his Marguerite, but in love with a friend who loved him back. At first it was sudden and difficult for family members to accept, thinking it would take longer to let go of Marguerite. Nothing they said would change his mind. He married Kay within just a few months. Kay was a bride again, and the details of planning the wedding and reception were delightful.

One detail she did not have to tend to was the reception centerpiece design. Woody guaranteed he would provide something appropriate and it was to be a secret. After the ceremony, the newlyweds were presented in the reception hall and on each table, Kay saw Woody's surprise.

Each center was their perfume . . . a jelly jar filled with water and rose petals.

Pam

Mothers wear many hats, and Pam has confidence and experience in every role. She is on the high seas of parenting four school-age children. Her tote bag is equipped with band aids, lip gloss, sunscreen, granola bars, paper and pens, hair bands, hand wipes, and just about anything that a bustling family may need. Her SUV has a supply of water bottles and snacks. It is apparent that her days revolve around her calendar and lists.

Pam is in the driver's seat multiple times daily, juggling pick-up and drop-off schedules to schools, dance practice, orthodontist appointments, and farmers' markets. She has periods of "curbside" waiting that allow her to read her book, catch up on her calendar, or nap.

Weekends are frequently filled with sports or dance competitions out of town. That is the time to pack the food, gear, and finally the kids. These are chaotic times, but the trips are fun, and time passes quickly. With all eight seats filled, kids chat away at high speed and volume. As the food and drinks are passed around, the rising noise level doesn't faze Pam. She loves the energy and silliness in the backseats as long as they are all safe and buckled up. "It will all happen too quickly," she says, as she thinks about them growing up and becoming independent.

As she loads up the kids and sees that they are all settled with seatbelts fastened, she checks her list and mirrors. She thinks about stretching one more time before taking her place in the driver's seat and turns the key. Her hands are at the helm, steering the pack to the next activity. With a spirit of love and gratitude for her dear cargo, a sense of privilege and grace, Pam embraces these precious moments that leave fingerprints on the SUV's windows and fingerprints on her heart.

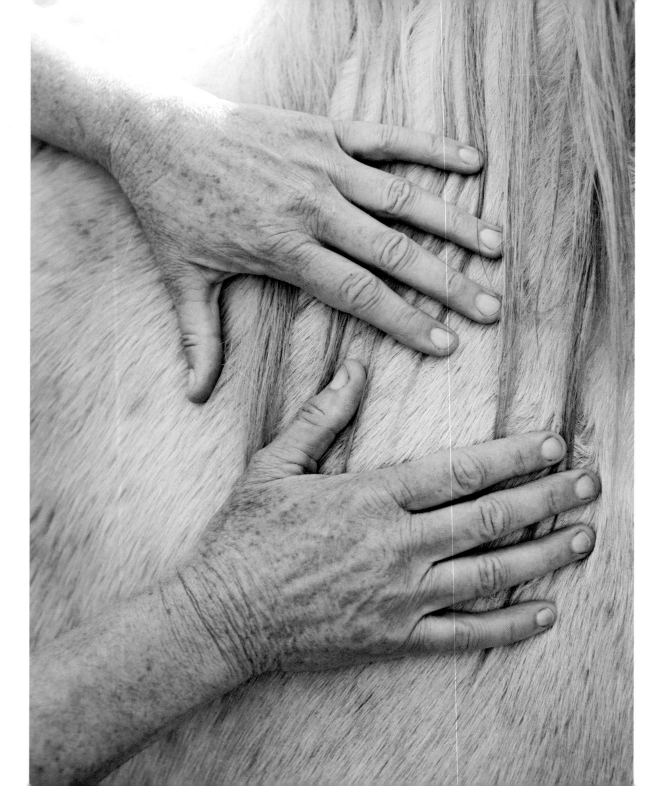

Diane

"Pistol was for sale," she says, speaking of the beautiful sorrel gelding in the pasture, "He was being sold for dog food, and Rosie needed a stable mate." Certainly, Diane had been one of those children who would come home with stray cats or dogs and beg, "Please, can I keep him?" She has a big heart for the rejected and has a home and acreage to match. Since the abused Pistol has found his home, he has gained a deep trust for Diane and is becoming more at ease with strangers. He and Rosie, the mare, find comfort in each other and in the safety of the healing environment that Diane and her husband, Ed, have created for them.

It was rewarding to discover that Diane's knowledge and expertise as a physical therapist would be able to help Pistol. Diane would regularly and gently treat his ailing body and lame leg with massage and therapeutic tools. He began to respond with gradual healing, and affection toward Diane. Over time his body actually expelled a large splinter of wood about the size of a pencil from his leg. His lameness was cured and in time the wounds in his soul would heal.

Most of Diane's patients are people. They arrive with their stressed and tight muscles, stiff joints, and the accumulation of worry and injury. She is a patient healer, a good listener—gentle, strong, and tenacious. Her sense of humor makes the work lighter, but as an advocate of balance and health, her wisdom is unshakeable. Her long, wavy, graying hair is pulled easily back into a ponytail and her skin is warmly tanned from the outdoors. She exudes a natural beauty that tempers any clinical tone in her medical art.

Although she loves her human clients, horses and dogs have been Diane's passion for decades. As she takes Pistol for a morning ride on the beach, she absorbs his gift to her . . . his affection, energy, and spirit. This horse, once considered dog food, became a treasured friend . . . restored and renewed with the touch of her hand.

Nick and Elizabeth

The sound of the skateboards repeatedly flying up and down the homemade ramp signaled that the boys were back. Stoked on skating, all of them between the ages of eleven and thirteen, none of them paid much attention to Elizabeth, the sixth grade brainiac little sister. None, except for Nick.

In the summer before eighth grade, Elizabeth discovered her love of surfing. It was easy for her to join the boys in their early morning and afterschool surfing ritual. In a few short years, Elizabeth became successful in surfing contests from Santa Cruz to San Onofre.

By high school, Nick realized his growing fondness for Elizabeth, and he secretly hoped one day he might date her. His mother recognized the look in his eye when they would see Elizabeth on her daily run. "Why don't you date Elizabeth?" she asked. He knew it might be awkward since Elizabeth's brother was his best friend, and she had had a boyfriend for over two years.

Despite her boyfriend, Elizabeth enjoyed meeting Nick for a surf session. Their friendship held a constant familiarity and affection throughout the early college years, but it started to feel like that was not enough. One day Elizabeth found a beautiful single lily on the windshield of her car. Elizabeth's hopes were realized when she found it was from Nick. The lily was a beginning of something new.

They decided, with the possibility of losing the friendship, to see where the future would take them. These two friends are still best friends and newlyweds. They support each other's dreams. Elizabeth is immersed in her Ph.D program and teaching, and Nick works full-time while pursuing a second career as a graphic artist. They still share a morning surf together. They are building a foundation to a future together, with trust and open hearts.

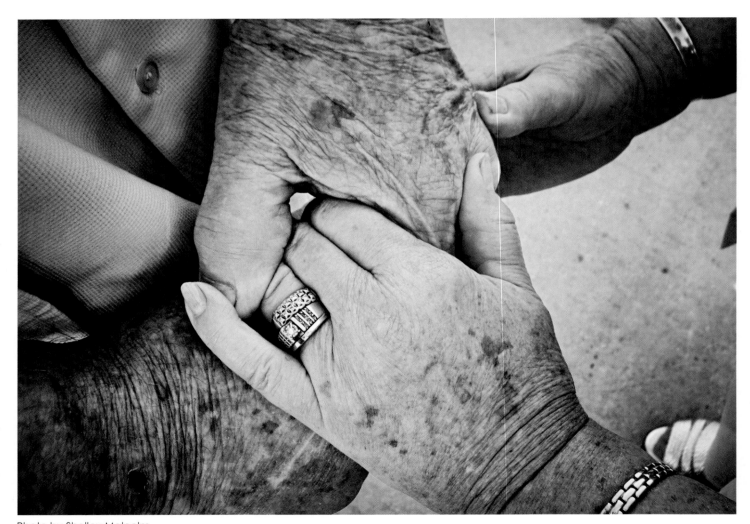

Photo by Shelley Malcolm

Bob and Shirley

As he steadies his balance with the best grip he can get on his cane, Bob clasps the gentle hands of his dear Shirley. Their wristwatches symbolize the importance of time. They have had almost sixty years together, six children, many grandchildren, and now great-grandchildren.

He still has the broad lumberjack build of a Minnesota farmer. Petite Shirley is even smaller with age, but there is a strength from within her that has rehabilitated Bob from the stroke. Somehow she has been able to keep up her household routine with the same love for setting the table and feeding a large family as she has for decades. Shirley is Bob's extra hands and caretaker. Bob has had to let go of some of his masculine pride so that his wife can lovingly button his buttons, click his seatbelt, and drive them to appointments or church. There is a shared sense of humor between them and the bantering just makes the adjustment easier.

He was the head of the house, driving trucks and huge farm equipment. She was the full-time mom, with an assortment of aprons for time spent in the kitchen. There were cows to milk, eggs to gather, gardens to tend. Days began with the sunrise and were long and full. There were the seasons for plowing and planting, summertime fishing and mosquitoes, and the long, dark, cold winters.

From the beginning, their journey has been one of side-by-side togetherness. This season of their life together has brought them to a different daily routine. They end each day with a precious ritual. Bob must sleep in a hospital bed and Shirley has a bed adapted to her weakening knees. They share the same room with their beds close together. They take each other's hand, give thanks for a wonderful rich life and they pray for loved ones. Hands clasped, they fall asleep.

Epilogue

Courage

Caesar moved to Colorado, then Nebraska, and learned how to do email. Shortly after, he learned to deal with email fraud as someone hacked his account. He hopes to earn his PhD .

Ceo has found her little apartment with its sunny, turreted windows. She is still settling in and volunteering at the YMCA where she loves to do yoga.

Kaz is looking forward to Brycen's wedding to beautiful fiancé, and cancer survivor, Marian.

Jamaine is serving the homeless at a community kitchen.

Hope

Ken works as a website manager with a voice operated program. **Mary** has become a wedding coordinator.

Fran passed away during summer 2009, not long after her son's wedding.

Davey faces his new life ahead and is helping his son and daughter-in-law build their first home.

Chet broke a leg and was diagnosed with throat cancer, but is determined to keep on painting and being independent. He still paints and lives alone.

Vicky, a chef at the local country club, loves days at the beach with her dog.

Renewal

Laura works part-time, but travels as much as she can . . . just returned from Washington D.C. and helped out in New Orleans with the Red Cross.

Chung has become successful with not only her magazine, but website and graphic design. She is a master at social networking.

Mary Ellen is an honors student and will have her degree in a year, and is rarely seen without her laptop computer.

Joan has enjoyed recent reunions with her sisters.

Work

Amy is newly engaged to long-time love, Jesse. She is producing a brand new wine this season.

Brian is proud to be nearly debt free. He hopes to get his degree soon.

Terry and daughter moved back to Michigan.

Candy is writing her own book on organizing.

Doug, successful in both professions, is becoming more interested in the Bible and taking time for walks.

Shelly's income is an anchor for her family at this time. She is glad she loves her work.

Tom sold the sandwich shop. The neighborhood misses him.

Dreams

Genae is pursuing a license in Massage Therapy.

Aaron is on the film festival circuit with the success of his first feature film, and is cast as a lead in a new film.

David is off to South Africa and Tahiti soon, but misses home more and more, where he has a vegetable garden and the surf is only four blocks away.

Meredith, Kelly, Carly, Trevor and Mike are in college, are realizing their interests and lives may not always keep them close together. However, they are the generation has grown up with their cell phones, so they are never more than a text, a call, or e message away.

Robin's first child leaves for college this fall.

Balance

Lynn's best friend of 40 years just passed away. She is spending more time at the beach house.

Betty is still travelling . . . making an attempt at not working so hard.

Jane just received a signed pencil drawing of her that was done in 1939. She and the artist met for the first time and returned the favor with a signed photo.

Cathy has a new role as new grandma and loves it.

Danny's wife passed away. Danny has gotten his teeth fixed and is selling his artwork in community shows.

Inspiration

Daniel has become a devout minister and has started his own church. He finds satisfaction in hard work . . . and fishing.

Randy and **Patty** are proud grandparents of toddlers, travel globally to serve in mission trips.

Lloyd and Sandy renewed their wedding vows.

Lois invented two new toys and helped to create an intricate educational puppet booth for earth day. She keeps the tennis courts busy, even at 80.

Kim now has several kittens and celebrated paying off her car.

Wisdom and Acceptance

Carol celebrated her 50th wedding anniversary year with Neil.

Kallie has started an inspirational online blog. She is traveling a lot.

Heather has found her passion in interior design, after years of musical theater.

Eileen loves living near her grown children who look in on her everyday and grows the most prolific flowering cacti around.

Gladys is staying healthy and close to church friends.

Purpose

Terri Lea climbed Machu Picchu.

George, in his 80s, is replacing the fascia boards on the eves of his house ... all by himself.

Suzanne balances her charity, business, and fun while she and her husband adjust to retirement.

Life

Ray has resigned from driving a car. Their daughter, Jean, is at the helm.

Steve is enjoying a transition in his route . . . new families and children moving in. His thumbs are getting tired.

Robert bought a house moved to the beach. He wore his Greek fishing hat, instead of cowboy hat at church.

Jim and Garin lost their beloved Labrador this year. It wasn't too long before a puppy stole their hearts.

Love

Kay and Woody are in love with gardening, traveling, and each other.

Diane continues her healing art and rides on the beach.

Nick and Elizabeth participated in rally and protests against hate crimes at her college. They surf as much as they can. Elizabeth has published her first book.

Pam now works with her husband in real estate. Three of her children are driving now.

Bob and Shirley continue to live on the old farm surrounded by family.

Acknowledgements

Thank you to all of the people who allowed us to use their hands and honest stories in this project. You are brave, inspiring, and beautiful.

Thank you to editors and supporters: Karen Grencik, Cindy Correa-Liebo, Joan Malcolm, Merrily Boult, Elizabeth Sine, Brady Teufel, Carol Wilcox, Terri Ikeda, Joette Eisengart, Jackie Starr, Jenny Malott and in Los Angeles: Lynn Lamoine, Lorena Batres-Jimenez, and Julie F DeLosReyes. Your patience and expertise humble me. In London, thank you to Jean Oelwang and the Marquesa de Varela. Thank you loved ones who know more about what they are doing than I do when it comes to dreaming big including Grace McGuire and her L10-E aircraft, Muriel. Thank you to my wonderful family.

Thank you to an awesome God. *Shelley*

Thank you Shelley, for bringing me along side of you and allowing me to be part of such an amazing project. Thank you Ryan, for supporting and encouraging me to fully follow my dream as a photographer. Many thanks to my family and friends who continually believe in and walk this journey with me. *Terilee*

Shelley Malcolm and Terilee Dawn Ouimette

Author and artist, **Shelley Malcolm** is co-owner of La Perla del Mar Chapel, in Shell Beach, which has become a destination for weddings, surf films, and other events, drawing guests from all over the world. Shelley has run marathons, hiked the Inca Trail to Machu Picchu, and created set designs for film, opera, and theater, including Les Miserables, Little Shop of Horrors, CATS, and the world premier of Tumbleweed Connection. Educated at UC Santa Barbara and UC Los Angeles, Shelley graduated from the University of Southern California. She is a mother of four, dental hygienist, community and church volunteer. Shelley Malcolm finds rest and inspiration at her beachside home in San Luis Obispo County, California.

Terilee Ouimette has loved art, people, and traveling from a very young age. Photography has been a great medium to combine her passions. She loves a good adventure, whether it is in Asia, Europe, or the Middle East. She has walked ruins dating back to Biblical times; eaten snake in Vietnam, ridden slides down the mountains of Switzerland and snowboarded in the beautiful Rocky Mountains of Canada where she grew up. She runs Terilee Dawn photography, hates cooking, loves her Converse shoes and could read all day. She has been married for 6 years and is expecting her first child. She can't wait to see where life takes her next.